Living Words

Sh'ma שמע

Since Rabbi Eugene Borowitz founded *Sh'ma* in 1970, the journal has served as a gathering place for independent voices eager to be heard across the Jewish religious, social, and political landscape. The pages of *Sh'ma* serve as a public diary of the North American Jewish experience, offering lively discussion on topics that cut to the very core of our Jewish sense of self. Our tactic is dialogue — rich conversation that embraces differing views, presented in an honest, respectful, and purposeful way. We seek to bring all of our readers to the table of sacred conversation. We cover topics as diverse as the politics of gender, trends in new Jewish social and political involvement, questions of culture and personal identity, ritual innovation, and new readings of ancient texts. Our readers are like our authors: sharp, seeking, concerned, and caring.

Share your voice with the *Sh'ma* family on our website: *www.Shma.com.*

Living Words

A Spiritual Source Book for an Age of Terror

Including a Selection of High Holiday Sermons from 5762

Edited with an Introduction by Susan Berrin

Foreword by David Saperstein

Sh'ma

Library of Congress Cataloging-in-Publication Data
        Sh'ma
            Living Words IV: A Spiritual Source Book for an Age of Terror
            ISBN 0-9664306-0-3

10 9 8 7 6 5 4 3 2 1

Contents

HIGH HOLIDAY REFLECTIONS

Acknowledgments

This book came about in great measure as a response to the tragic and sobering events of September 11, 2001. As a writer and editor, I was fortunate to have a specific role upon which to focus my attention during the hours and days immediately following the collapse of the World Trade Center towers. In my work, I had a place to pour the sadness, grief, and terror; hopelessness was replaced with mission. Rosh Hashanah followed the terrorist attacks within a week, and as sermons began to arrive by email, I realized that they all spoke to the events of September 11. The words I read made evident a deep longing to make sense of tragedy, to probe, to wrestle with God, to be comforted, to take the opportunity of gathering as a community to find solace with each other.

Published as a memorial to Charles Alan Zion, who was killed in the collapse of the World Trade Center, *Living Words IV* is meant to serve as a resource for rabbis and teachers as well as a source of comfort as we approach the anniversary of the attack, the first *yahrzeit*, and the High Holidays of 5763. I decided to broaden the initial *Living Words* mandate of publishing only sermons, and have included essays that appeared originally in the December 2001 issue of *Sh'ma*, as well as new writings about fighting terrorism and talking with children in the wake of tragedy.

In past years I have approached *Living Words* as a record: What issues were facing us at the High Holidays? What were rabbis and *darshanim* teaching on the holiest of Jewish days? It is our intention that the 10 sermons collected here — chosen from among the nearly 100 considered for this volume —

will not only record a moment in history but will offer inspiration that enables us to face horror with dignity and sorrow in community.

Like all collections of words between two covers, this book is given life through the efforts of many people. My thanks to Erica Ernst, who was the Office and Projects Coordinator at Jewish Family & Life! during the time much of the work on this book was done, and helped shepherd the collection in its earliest stages. Josh Eagle has very ably continued that process. Several members of the Jewish Family & Life! staff were involved in the process of selecting the sermons, reading and proofreading the typeset pages, including Harry Bloom, Judy Bolton-Fasman, and Martha Hausman. The *Sh'ma* Advisory Committee includes several very devoted readers and contributors. Their suggestions give depth to the pluralistic and textured conversations we create in the journal. I'd like to thank Neil Gillman, who chairs the committee, as well as Jack Bieler, Jeremy Burton, Nina Beth Cardin, Aryeh Cohen, Shoshana Gelfand, Caroline Harris, Hadar Harris, Phil Miller, Jennie Rosenn, Jonathan Schreiber, and Carl Sheingold. A special appreciation to the publisher, Yosef I. Abramowitz, who nurtures and champions *Sh'ma* with a serious dedication and effervescent passion.

For 32 years, *Sh'ma* has built a community of readers among the intellectual, religious, cultural, and communal Jewish leadership of North America. Its pages are filled monthly with essays that inspire social change and enlarge the table at which Jews sit with one another in dialogue. Maintaining this community of readers and writers is both a challenge and a source of great satisfaction. May these writings teach us more about ourselves and others, and may they help us along the path to greater tolerance, so that our lives and the lives of those who died on September 11 may be lived and remembered as a blessing.

Susan Berrin
Editor
May 2002
Iyar 5762

Foreword

By David Saperstein

The history of every nation and every people is marked by cataclysmic events that define their character and shape their history. September 11 may well turn out to be such a moment for the American people, shattering, as it did, America's sense of invulnerability in our own land and requiring a response to international phenomena reflecting powerful political, religious, ethnic, and cultural dynamics. When such crises have occurred over the centuries, the Jewish communities touched by them have also responded. We see those responses in sermons, historical writings, ritual, liturgies, and new modalities to convey the meaning of such events to adults and children — refracting such events through the lens of Jewish values, Jewish security, and Jewish politics.

American Jews, of course, experienced these events both as Americans and as Jews. This remarkable compilation of sermons and essays on *halachah*, history, politics, ritual, and pedagogy articulates distinctive, and still evolving, Jewish responses to September 11. This is how it has always been. The seder, the menorah, the sukkah are all Jewish symbols upon which each generation imprints its distinctive quest for spiritual meaning.

The outlines of a Jewish interpretation and response to September 11 are becoming clear. First, the writings in this volume reflect a phenomenon that marked this nation's response to September 11: a pronounced turn to religion, religious language, and worship. It was to our synagogues, churches, temples, and mosques — and to religious leaders and thinkers — that so many Americans turned for comfort, community, and context. Across the nation, on September 11, rabbis tore up carefully crafted Rosh Hashanah sermons, educators revamped their curricula, and Jewish leaders and organizations revised their policy agendas. As these writings reflect, American Jews (and others) overwhelmingly found what they were looking for.

Second, Jews noted with irony that Americans began to understand more clearly what Israelis have been living with for many years: extremists who target a civilian population simply for the crime of being who and where they are.

Third, Israel's model of civilian vigilance and responsibility, and its efforts at targeting terrorists, became the paradigm of an American response to terrorism. Bittersweet lessons for America emerge from the Israeli model: the enormous success in staying the hand of terrorists along with the attendant failure to stop all terrorists; the accuracy of Israel's efforts along with the faulty intelligence and military errors that have taken many innocent lives; Israel's defiance of the terrorists' efforts to destroy the Israeli will and its vibrant civic and democratic structures along with the attendant compromises Israel has made in its struggle for civil liberties.

Fourth, America acknowledged that military action must be part of any effective response toward terrorism. While the Jewish community remains as liberal as ever according to most demographic polls, it has also been a strong advocate (e.g. in Kuwait, Bosnia and Kosovo) for the use of military force for the purpose of protecting innocent victims. Two sources drive this paradoxical view: Jewish history, replete as it is with the tragedies that have befallen us because good people remained silent in the face of evil; and our legal texts that affirm that force can be used morally — but must never become an end in itself. Jewish guidelines of what Christians call "just war" theory set norms and limits on that use of force and remind us that force alone will never be an adequate answer to the complex religious, economic, political, and cultural causes that underlay the plague of terrorism today. Arguably, we have not yet been as outspoken and assertive in addressing the non-military challenges of applying, in public discourse and policy terms, the values contained in these essays and sermons. This remains an urgent challenge to America's Jews.

Fifth, too many Americans are ignoring an unmistakable lesson of our history — that curtailment of freedoms and rights in times of crisis comes back to haunt us (the internment of Japanese Americans, for example). How often were attacks on Jews justified or tolerated because of fear? We must carefully balance new law enforcement authority to combat terrorism with the preservation of our fundamental freedoms. This balancing is difficult — all the more so when passions are understandably enflamed. Here, I'm afraid, our communal response was too timid. Our eagerness to see America finally stand up to terrorism led us to come late to the defense of civil liberties, and the discussion was less textured for our absence. Alas, we will have many opportunities to play a more active role in this vital debate.

Sixth, Jews, who have often been victimized by group hatred, know well how destruction can be wrought in the name of religiously and politically justified hatred. While we call for a strong response to terrorism, we have also been among the strongest voices denouncing group hatred against Muslims, Arabs, and Sikhs and other Southeast Asians who resemble Arabs.

Finally, most of the sermons in this collection were written in the immediate aftermath of the events and were aimed at interpreting the events of September 11 for a still traumatized community. Jews everywhere were struck by the power and mystery of the words of one of the central and most powerful prayers of our High Holy Day liturgy: *"Unetanah tokef k'dushat ha-yom ki hu norah va-yom."* "Let us proclaim the sacred power of this day, it is awesome and full of dread.... On Rosh Hashanah it is written, on Yom Kippur it is sealed: how many will pass on, how many shall come to be? Who shall live and who shall die? Who shall live to see ripe age and who shall perish? Who by fire and who by water? Who by sword and who by beast?" The prayer culminates, *"U'teshuvah, u'tefilah u'tzedakah ma'avirin et ro'ah ha-g'zeirah,"* often translated, "But repentance, prayer, and charity will avert judgment's severe decree."

We know that the victims of September 11 did nothing to deserve their fates, yet the severe decree was not averted for them. The targeted planes and buildings were filled with innocent people. Too often, great trauma, whether personal or communal, can poison, embitter, and fill us with self-pity. It can paralyze and lead us to denial, resulting in righteous indignation.

The terrorists who sought to undermine our national will, our civic norms, and our freedoms will not prevail. The extraordinary charity of the American people, governmental determination to learn the policy lessons of this historic event, and religious gatherings marking our nation's response began the long and difficult path that we, as a nation and a community, will in the end travel.

David Saperstein is Director of the Religious Action Center of Reform Judaism.

Introduction

By Susan Berrin

Sometimes a good book begins simply as a way to answer questions. Sometimes a good book simply puts those questions into a public arena. In the days immediately after September 11, and the months that have followed, we have had to wrestle with an array of questions that are at once moral and geopolitical; questions that are biblical and contemporary; questions that are legal and religious.

September 11 was a day that intruded on the consciousness of the world, completely and indelibly marking the lives of Americans as well as global citizens. It continues to impact our lives, both in the ordinary ways we inhabit the universe and in the extraordinary ways we think about universal moral principles. The acts of terrorism unsettled our rhythms. It unsettled our complacency. It challenged our spiritual leaders who were preparing for the High Holidays. The anticipated anthology of High Holiday sermons, *Living Words IV* became much more than a collection of holiday teachings. While sermons still spoke about *tshuvah* and themes of renewal, they were located emotionally in the horrors of the terrorist attack. Dozens of *drashot* focused on a few simple but perplexing prayers, given greater meaning, irony, and power against the backdrop of September 11.

What does it mean to unsettle our routines? Our certainties? Altering the content, the anticipated focus, of a book is minor. The volume that now sits in your hands is the product of addressing both the certainties of life and, more important, the uncertainties of individual lives.

As we approach the High Holidays of 5763, as September 11, 2002 nears, so much feels changed, shaken. This is a time to take stock. It is a time to reflect not only on the horrific events of September 11, but on the reactions and responses of our communal and governmental leadership. Indelibly we are marked by September 11, 2001; but how will we approach the fall of 2002?

This source book is a resource for addressing the multitude of issues that arose post-9/11. There are essays on prayer in the wake of tragedy, essays that question the moral principles of war and its impact on civil liberties, and essays that offer guidance about how best to speak about these issues with our children — both at home and in the Jewish classroom.

Living Words IV: A Spiritual Source Book for an Age of Terror addresses the significant questions born of the terrorist attacks. We begin with one of the most important: Can wars be holy? Saul Berman, a leading voice of Modern Orthodoxy, delineates two types of war according to Jewish law. Unlike other religions, according to Berman, Judaism does not have a category of "just" or "holy" war. But we are compelled to fight evil — "the evil in the world [that] resides in particular persons." Noted speaker and author Marc Gopin writes about the relationship between this war and religion. He says, "Anyone who thinks [this war] is not about religion should take a good look at the document written by the terrorist mastermind Mohammed Atta." Describing the document as a preparation for death and afterlife, Gopin suggests that Islamic fundamentalists must look seriously at themselves. As well, we — Jews, Christians, and Muslims — must address the question of when violence is justified. A historical perspective on Jewish holy war ideas is the focus of Reuven Firestone's essay. Professor of Medieval Judaism and Islam at Hebrew Union College-Jewish Institute of Religion, Firestone exhorts that before dismissing "the appalling behavior of our Muslim cousins engaged in holy war, let us put our own house in order... We must neutralize if not eradicate the ugly and gravely dangerous revival of holy war within Judaism."

Michael Berenbaum, a Sh'ma Contributing Editor who has written extensively on the Holocaust, asks an essential question that surfaced immediately after the attacks: "Where was God? If God is not to be found in the act of commission or in the choice of victims, God is to be found amidst the rubble. If there is to be healing, God will be found amidst the ruins." Berenbaum continues, "The question is what to do with the very fact of survival ... The survivors ... will not be defined by the lives they have led until now, but the lives they will lead from now on." Drawing deeply on Holocaust sensibilities, he ends his essay poignantly: "For the experience of near death to have ultimate meaning, it must take shape in how one rebuilds from the ashes. Such for the individual; so too, for the nation."

Retired U.S. Navy Chaplain Arnold Resnicoff underscores that while fighting terrorism, Americans must uphold their values. Drawing on his experiences in Vietnam, he says, "I learned to value outrage because it reminded me I was still human ... Rage could destroy the humanity I still cherished. Rage destroys our moral compass."

His words are underscored by Under Secretary of Defense at the Pentagon Dov Zakheim. "As Jews and as Americans, we can and must retain our moral and ethical compass even

xvii

as we implement unconventional rules of war." An Orthodox Jew, Zakheim wrestles with "balancing the imperatives that drive a free society with the limitations on freedom that are necessarily imposed to maintain internal vigilance against a shadowy foe." Noted author, attorney, and civil libertarian Alan Dershowitz addresses this balance with his personal and thoughtful essay, "Rethinking Liberty in the Age of Terrorism." Acknowledging the inherent dangers of governmental information gathering, he suggests opening this and other security-related liberty issues to public debate. Rethinking his own position on several of these issues, he says, "It is far better for everybody to be deprived of a little bit of anonymity than for one specific ethnic group to bear a disproportionate part of the burden."

Dawn Rose, who directed the Reconstructionist Rabbinical School's Ethics Center, argues that Judaism prohibits using the public's ignorance against itself. Her essay challenges the Bush Administration on its public selling of the war, stating that "the message is that peacetime rules, of necessity, must be suspended ... that rules developed through painful past history about human rights during wartime might not apply." Rose's reflections on the power of words are sobering. She scrutinizes President Bush's equivocation between intended and unintended loss, concluding: "We must call death, death." Drawing upon moral lessons from the Holocaust, *Sh'ma* Contributing Editor Yitz Greenberg writes about the "ethics of power — how, when, and why to exercise force." He suggests that the hard lessons learned from Jewish history should be shared with Americans: "Evil must be confronted thoroughly and with force sufficient to defeat it."

Vanessa Ochs, another *Sh'ma* Contributing Editor and Director of Jewish Studies at the University of Virginia, and William Lebeau, Vice Chancellor at the Jewish Theological Seminary, share thoughts about the place of prayer in a time of tragedy. Ochs considers the difficulty of praying, a concern that our rush to words obscures "the condition we should be experiencing — a sense of horror." Lebeau sees prayer as "a natural response to that horror... Jewish tradition provides keen insight into the role of prayer in the human experience." We pray, he says, "to steel ourselves against the inclination to abandon our responsibility for repair of the world."

Jeffrey Spitzer, an educator, offers a prayer he wrote the evening after the attacks. Calling on the Source of Life to protect us, he also asks God to give us courage, compassion, and the understanding to not act out of fear or anger.

The High Holidays Reflections section includes teachings from Orthodox, Conservative, Reform, and Reconstructionist rabbis. These teachers offer comfort and understanding. They share stories and parables that unmask our anger, our hopelessness. Their sermons assert the importance of democracy and pluralism, an open society, pursuing an understanding of "the other," wrestling with our own violent and disturbing texts. They affirm the delicate balance between protecting civil liberties, living with fear, and the need to feel safe. They ask difficult questions: How do we fight a war without putting self-reflection and moral scrutiny aside? They help us reclaim hope, drawing both on our Jewish resources and our engagement with community.

Another section of *Living Words IV* includes educational materials for children and adults. Michael Balinsky, Director of Faculty Development at the Florence Melton Adult Mini-

School, offers detailed plans for an adult education class on confronting violence in Jewish texts. Working with troubling texts forces us to acknowledge the violence within our own sacred writings and approach the writings of other religions with more sensitivity. Sheryl Katz and Maxine Handelman of the Chicago Jewish Community Center, and Or Rose of the Jewish Community Day School of Boston, provide insights for parents and teachers to guide their work with children. Rose shares strategies from his day school experiences for teaching pluralism and tolerance. He says, "As a Jewish educator, I feel blessed to have a rich and varied storehouse of rituals, prayers, ideas, and texts to draw upon during times of pain and confusion."

Like Balinsky, David Elcott offers a curriculum that addresses questions of war in Jewish tradition. He provides a lesson plan for teaching children to discern between *milhemet mitzvah* (an obligatory war) and *milhemet reshut* (a discretionary war). Kathy Bloomfield completes the section with a list of books for children of all ages that focus on tolerance, peacemaking, coping with loss and trauma, and teaching Jewish ethics.

Living Words IV: A Spiritual Source Book for an Age of Terror is a resource for both Jews and Americans. *Sh'ma* Contributing Editor Brad Hirshfield, in an interview, commented that "Jews, in particular, are heirs to a tradition that shows us how to remain ethically aware without becoming politically and militarily paralyzed ... There is a real contribution that Jews can make to America because we have long understood that for the sake of building and preserving a society that embodies the ethical values we hold sacred, we are required to do things that are not always nice and not always pretty. But we also know that we have to do these things in a manner that remains self-aware and self-critical." This collection serves that mission: to ask difficult questions, to wrestle with ethical values, to remain self-aware and self-critical, and to use our Jewish heritage to help preserve a safe, pluralist, and democratic America.

A Prayer
By Jeffrey Spitzer

Lord,

Source of Life, Creator of all flesh,

From out of the depths we call unto you.

Protect us from the hand of all our enemies.

Comfort Your children who now stand alone without parent or brother or sister or child.

Strengthen us to stand with those orphaned by this attack on our country.

This country, our country, shelter of peace to the downtrodden, that has gathered in millions of the peoples of the world stands as a beacon of light and justice, but today is dimmed with horror and tragedy.

New York and Washington, shining cities, diminished like Jerusalem after the destruction of the holy Temple, need Your comfort, and our aid; help us to maintain our courage and our efforts to support our people.

Strengthen the hands of those who defend this country, and those who try to maintain peace against these attacks.

Teach us to speak to our children with love and support and courage and understanding, for we are all fearful, although their fears may not be our fears.

Gain for us a heart of wisdom, that we may act out of compassion and thoughtfulness, and not out of anger or prejudice.

Accept with mercy our prayers for our country and its government, its president, judges, officials, and institutions who faithfully toil for the good of our country.

May they, with Your guidance, lead us back to lives of peace in a land we have come to love.

Addressing a War on Terrorism

The War Against Evil and Ethical Constraints

Saul J. Berman

God is good, but there is evil in God's imperfect world.

J ewish law knows only two categories of war — those mandated by Torah and those that are discretionary, able to be initiated under the joint authority of King and Sanhedrin. There is no category such as "holy war" in Jewish thought because the taking of human life, while under limited circumstances permissible and sometimes even mandated, can never be *kadosh*, holy. In fact, the taking of human life always results in *tumah*, impurity, the presence of which is an absolute barrier to the presence of *kedushah*, holiness.

But the existence of both mandatory and discretionary wars in the Torah compels us to recognize that there can exist, in human nations and cultures, a level of corruption and evil that we are required to combat. We are not allowed to close our eyes in denial of such evil.

1

In recent weeks I have been hearing theological rationalizations that deny evil: God is good, therefore all events in the world must be good; we just don't understand the ultimate good purpose of apparently evil events. Maimonides considers and rejects this understanding of God's providence in the world on the ground that it is contradicted by both reason and revelation. Yes, God is good, but there is evil in God's imperfect world; God demands that we identify it in nature and in the exercise of human free will in order that we combat and overcome it. Indeed, the consequence of denying evil is acceptance of and passivity toward, instead of active resistance to, evil in the world.

The ethical relativism of those who argue that we must understand the Islamic fundamentalists' anger and fury, their willingness to visit death and destruction upon thousands of innocent people in order to do battle with the American "infidel," is another form of denial of evil. We are Jewishly duty-bound to repudiate such amelioration of individual responsibility for evil and murderous behavior. Jewish law does not allow taking the lives of innocent persons even in direct defense of one's own life. Rav Yehuda Amital, speaking during Sukkot at the Edah Conference in Israel, referred to the Islamic fundamentalists' position as a *chillul Hashem*, a desecration of God's name — our common God could not possibly reward an act of suicide done for the purpose of slaughtering innocent civilians!

If evil needs to be recognized and opposed, are there no limits to the methods we use?

The Torah mandates two wars of extermination. The first was the war against the seven Canaanite nations that occupied the Land of Israel at the time of the Exodus. The second was the war against Amalek. These two instances, in contrast even to mandatory wars of self-defense and to all forms of discretionary war, sanctioned taking the lives of civilian non-combatants.

In the early 1900s, Rabbi Chaim Soloveitchik of Brisk argued that, according to Maimonides, there was a possibility of contemporary war against Amalek — such as a national attempt to exterminate the Jewish people. His grandson, Rabbi Yosef Dov Soloveitchik, used this position in the early 1940s to contend that the Allied war against Nazi Germany could be understood in Jewish law as a war against Amalek. Rabbi Soloveitchik, of blessed memory, insisted, however, that the war against this new "figurative Amalek" was not subject to the same liberties vis-a-vis individual civilian vulnerability as was the war against the original Amalek. Rather, the usual moral constraints applicable even to a war of self-defense would apply in this war as well.

Maimonides recorded the accepted rabbinic position that those wars could be fought only against the specific peoples God identified as deserving of such extreme violence. When those nation-states disappeared, it was no longer permissible intentionally to engage in war against noncombatants.

In contrast to individual self-defense, national self-defense allows for preemptive strikes. Israel's preemptive strike against other nations in 1967 was unquestionably permissible according to Jewish law. While Jewish law would not generally condone political assassination, it would certainly allow the targeting for execution of persons who had already committed acts of homicide and who were believed to be engaged in planning further such acts. Such executions, undertaken by legitimate government rather than individuals, constitute part of the responsible exercise of national self-defense.

Nevertheless, even a nation, according to Jewish law, may not engage in the indiscriminate injuring or killing of non-combatants. Rabbi Aharon Soloveitchik, who recently passed away, expressed deep opposition to American policy during the war in Vietnam that allowed broad air attacks on civilian population centers in order to displace Vietcong units. Rav Aharon viewed such actions as a breach of the prohibition against homicide, not justified even in the conduct of an otherwise permissible war.

For individuals as for nations, the Torah demands balance between the responsibility to combat evil and the duty to preserve respect for all human life. An individual may take life in self-defense, but only the life of the actual aggressor. The government may utilize capital punishment, but must minimize its utilization to only the most certain of cases. A nation must sometimes go to war, but it must act in a manner that reduces the likelihood of indiscriminate death to non-combatants.

We need to admit that the presence of evil in the world resides in particular persons. We must be committed to combat such evil, even by war, in order to protect innocent persons and to promote just values in the world. But we must exercise care that we not abandon the very values that we seek to protect, in the attempt to make the world safe for those values. The balance is not easy to maintain, but consciousness of the duty to do so is critical to its achievement.

Rabbi Saul J. Berman is Director of Edah, a voice of Modern Orthodoxy. He also teaches at Stern College and Columbia University School of Law.

This War Is About Religion and Cannot Be Won Without It

Marc Gopin

The cruel nadir of some people's Islam must be fought in its own backyard.

The sooner we face facts, the more powerful our chances to succeed in making religious terrorism a temporary phenomenon of human culture. But we cannot do this if we hide our heads in the sand. Politically incorrect or not, this war is about religion. Anyone who thinks it is not about religion should take a good hard look at the document written by the terrorist mastermind of the World Trade Center bombing, Mohammed Atta, in order to help his soldiers prepare for their sanctified deaths. It is one of the most profound religious documents I have ever seen, and its preparation for a beautiful death and afterlife is so compelling that I almost forgot, as I read it transfixed, that it was really about mass murder. This death wish is a careful weaving of purification rituals to be accepted into Paradise, including asking God for forgiveness of sins! Mass murder is,

5

of course, not one of the sins in this unique reading of Islam. It is, on the contrary, a supreme religious act of struggle with the forces of evil. But the atrocity is not even mentioned by name. It is simply the struggle with evil. In fact, it is over-shadowed in the letter by the holy rituals of death preparations, as if a meditative concentration on Paradise is at the core of every act leading to the end, rather than revenge or murder.

The fact that terrorism defies what used to be thought of as the traditional Islamic laws pertaining to war is beside the point. The fact is that in the experiences of the thousands of people who have been on streets around the world screaming "Osama Bin Laden" in adulation, this was not an atrocity but a religious act. And they have many a cleric who has told them so. Shame on those clerics for betraying other moral principles of Islam, as well as universal principles of justice and compassion.

What is to be done? Counterterrorism? Massive development and poverty alleviation efforts for the Middle East? A complete revamping of relationships with regimes that keep most people absurdly poor in the Middle East? The answer is a resounding yes to all of these efforts. Are they enough? No. The reason is simple. We cannot change hearts and minds in the long run with threats and counteraggression. And we cannot buy off an ideology with jobs and money. We certainly can make the good life more tempting and attainable for millions more people. And we must do that. But this barbaric ideology, this cruel nadir of some people's Islam is a phenomenon that must be fought in its own backyard. The offensive must be taken against the barbarity of Islamicism — Islamic fundamentalism — rather than Islamic religion and high culture. And no one can do this ultimately but Muslims themselves. But we Jews can help in some significant ways.

We should help initiate a conversation on religious limits in the use of violence. This will be a hard discussion, because it directly affects attitudes toward Israel's use of force. On an internal level, we must look at when and how violence is justified by Judaism. I have argued elsewhere that the Jewish "just war" tradition, and the "just war" traditions of the other monotheisms, in principle, cannot justify much in the way of war, due to collateral damage — the killing of noncombatants. But all traditions change, and we are witnessing a complete repudiation of this principle in the hands of today's leading Middle Eastern Muslim clerics. In fact, when the goal is "justified," such as the liberation of Muslim lands, they seem to be declaring suicidal, terrorist targeting of noncombatants as martyrdom.

Goal-oriented justification of mass murder of noncombatants is inherently evil. In Jewish tradition we must emphasize *pikuach nefesh*, the saving and protection of innocent life, as the ultimate arbiter of difficult decisions about war and violence. We must avoid at all costs behavior in war and conflict that leads to the injury and death of innocents. The deliberate and purposeful murder of noncombatants is *retzihah*, a violation of the Ten Commandments.

This is the bridge upon which traditional Jews can travel, meet, challenge, and hopefully join forces with Islamic and Christian contemporaries. There may be some "blow back" regarding Israel, but this ethical standard is one that the vast majority of Israelis would embrace.

We must find more ways to embrace Muslims willing to search for a just peace between Israelis and Palestinians. I

have many such Muslim friends. And we must agree to dis-
agree with other Muslims who wrongly believe in violent
resistance, but who could repudiate the terrorist essence of
Hamas and Islamic Jihad. This agreement on the limits of
war practices is crucial to the eventual settlement of the
Israeli-Palestinian conflict, as well as to victory over those
Islamic forces who are threatening the very stability of
Western civilization.

We must build coalitions with beleaguered liberal
Muslims for the sake of human rights, democracy, and the
basic freedoms of a civil society — distinguishing between
the needs and desires of Muslims and Islamicists. Islamicists
want control of public space, through violence if necessary.
They can be isolated if we, in the U.S. and in Israel, honor
Muslims and treat them with utmost dignity. In the long run
we will have a hard time existing on this planet unless Islam
is reclaimed from the Islamicists. To do that, we will be
compelled to address behavior that is out of bounds for
humanity.

———

*Rabbi Dr. Marc Gopin is Visiting Associate Professor of
International Diplomacy and Senior Researcher at the Fletcher
School at Tufts University, and author of* Between Eden and
Armageddon: The Future of World Religions, Violence, and
Peacemaking, *as well as the forthcoming* Holy War, Holy Peace.
*He is currently a Visiting Scholar at the Program on Negotiation
at Harvard University.*

Our Own House Needs Order

Reuven Firestone

---

*We must neutralize, if not eradicate, the ugly
and dangerous revival of holy war within
Judaism.*

A couple of years ago I proudly showed my new book, *Jihad: The Origin of Holy War in Islam*, to a Muslim colleague of mine, trained with a Ph.D. in an American university, and now the head of the Department of Contemporary Islamic Studies at al-Quds University in Jerusalem. He took one look at the title and turned to me with a look of pity and almost disgust on his face. "Reuven," he said, "you must know that there is no holy war in Islam!" And there is no holy war in Judaism.

Fighting — as we learn from Rabbi Saul Berman — is not *kadosh*. Neither is it *muqaddas*, as my Muslim scholar friend told me. But if God commands war, if the authority to engage in fighting and inevitably mass killing is divinely inspired, is the act sanctified? "Holy war," with all its connotations of mindless excess, fervent, and wild fanaticism, is not a

9

Christian monopoly; the sooner Jews and Muslims acknowledge this fact, the better.

We Jews observe the acts and rhetoric coming from al-Qa'ida, Hamas, and Islamic Jihad and we know that *qital* (warring), or *jihad* (exerting great effort), or *fi sabil Allah* (in the path of God) is holy war. While such warring in Islam is governed by rational and ethical rules of engagement, just as "just war" theory in the West is governed by such rules (*jus ad bellum, jus in bello*), excess always abounds when the warrior knows that the cause or authority for fighting transcends the rationale or logic of the human mind. The ecstasy of personal sacrifice in obeying God's will, of willingness literally to obliterate the self in the ultimate sacrifice of giving one's own life to the divine command, may lead to extraordinary valor or extraordinary atrocity.

Before dismissing the appalling behaviors of our Muslim cousins engaged in holy war, let us put our own house in order. Holy war has been revived among Israel the people and within Israel the state. Why is *milhemet mitzvah/hovah* obligatory war? Because God-the-Commander (*ha-Metzaveh*) requires it. Is it not a holy act to carry out God's command? Is there not an essence of *kedushah* in the fulfillment of every mitzvah, large or small? When the rabbis in *Mishnah Sotah* 8:7 categorized Israel's wars as obligatory or discretionary, they were attempting to define and dismiss a dangerous phenomenon that had twice in their memory brought devastation to the Jewish people. Both the great Revolt of 66 C.E. and the Bar Kokhba Rebellion of 132 C.E. — two of the most horrific and catastrophic events that the Jewish people ever experienced — were driven by Jewish holy war ideas.

After the *Mishnah*, Jewish holy war ideas lay virtually dormant for most of our exilic existence, though they were discussed briefly by certain medieval thinkers and appear in some of our apocalyptic and messianic writings. But holy war has been revived in contemporary Israel, especially among ultranationalist Orthodox settlers in Judea and Samaria (the West Bank) and their many supporters. The war — and it may now be accurately called a war between Israel and the Palestinians — is defined by many religiously observant settlers and their supporters as a divine obligation to reclaim the whole of the Land of Israel, as either a prelude to or actually part of the messianic awakening. Many in this camp cite ad nauseum the now famous statement of Nahmanides in his gloss on Maimonides' *Book of Commandments* (positive commandment 4), who teaches that the conquest and settlement of the Land of Israel lies in the category of obligatory war (*milhemet mitzvah*). "It is a positive commandment for all generations obligating every individual, even during the period of exile."

As Jewish holy war has entered religious and political discourse in relation to the Israel-Palestine conflict, so has the increase of Jewish atrocities in the name of a higher cause. It reached its peak in the mid-1980s to mid-1990s with the maiming and murder of Muslim noncombatants by the Jewish Underground, the massacre of Muslims in prayer by Baruch Goldstein, and Yigal Amir's assassination of Prime Minister Yitzhak Rabin. Holy war ideas continue to inform the behavior of many religious settlers to this day, though there has been a concerted effort by both the Israeli government and the settler movement to refrain from committing such blatant atrocities.

Radical Muslim terrorists maim and kill in the name of

God, perverting the normative Islamic legal traditions in their self-proclaimed justification for the mass slaughter of innocents. Where are the imams and other Muslim religious leaders who should be condemning these hideous acts? And while we have the right to ask where these voices are, we will have little impact on the complex internal debates that confront the Muslim communities in this country and the rest of the world. Holy war is a dangerous reality. We have now felt its sting. Let us, therefore, before we try vainly and patronizingly to intervene in the internal debates of another religious community, put our own house in order. We must neutralize if not eradicate the ugly and gravely dangerous revival of holy war within Judaism. The first step is to acknowledge its existence. The next is to engage in public discussion *within our own community*, especially among the spectrum of religious leaders, to mitigate the inherently self-destructive and ultimately immoral efforts to define our fighting with the Palestinians as a holy war.

Reuven Firestone is Professor of Medieval Judaism and Islam at Hebrew Union College in Los Angeles. He has authored Journeys in Holy Lands: The Abraham-Ishmael Legends in Islam *(SUNY, 1990),* Jihad: The Origin of Holy War in Islam *(Oxford, 1999),* Children of Abraham: An Introduction to Judaism for Muslims *(Ktav, 2001), and dozens of articles on Islam and its relations with Judaism and Christianity.*

In Judaism, There Are Always Rules

Dov S. Zakheim

As Jews and as Americans, we can and must retain our moral and ethical compass even as we implement unconventional rules of war.

For the first time in living memory, Jewish Americans have been victimized by terrorism in their own backyards. This experience is hardly a novelty to Israelis, for whom terrorist attacks on civilians sadly have become a daily occurrence. Nor is it a new experience for Jews in general. Jews have experienced terrorism of one sort or another ever since the Amalekites attacked the weakest civilian elements of the Israelite camp.

Like all other aspects of Jewish life, that first war against terror was governed by divine guidelines, though very unconventional ones. In general, the Israelites conducted their military operations under strict rules of engagement. They were prohibited from attacking foes who were prepared to sue for peace — from engaging in wanton rape, even from destroying the fruit trees of conquered lands.

13

These and other restrictions injected a sense of civility, morality, and ethics even when facing an enemy on the battlefield.

In contrast, the prescribed biblical response to Amalek's depredations went much further: the Israelites were commanded to destroy Amalek root and branch. When King Saul failed to kill the Amalekites "and utterly destroy all that they have, both man and woman, infant and suckling, ox and sheep . . ." — or even kill their king, Saul forfeited his own kingdom. The prophet Samuel tolerated neither half-measures nor excuses.

Nevertheless, what was common to both conventional and unconventional warfare in ancient Israel was the fact that the rules of engagement reflected higher values, not merely human emotion. That fact remains valid today, both in Israel and, as terrorism has spread to the United States, in this country as well.

A recent *halachic* debate in Israel underscores this proposition. A strict reading of the *halachic* texts would seem to imply that a terrorist may be summarily killed after, as well as during, a firefight without intervening judicial procedure. Yet, as Rabbi Yehuda Henkin has argued in numerous writings, two additional and critical considerations also apply.

First, there is the issue of *dina demalchuta dina* —"the law of the kingdom is the law." International law, like American law, indeed like Israeli law, prevents the killing of captured terrorists, despite the impulse to do so.

Second, for Israel, but perhaps not only for Israel, there is the issue that the killing of unarmed prisoners would result in *chilull Hashem*, the profanation of the Divine Name. While the United States is not governed by *halachah*, it does purport to be acting in God's name — the God of Jews as well as of

Christians, Muslims, Sikhs, and others. To kill imprisoned or captured terrorists would, therefore, besmirch the divinity in the eyes of nonbelievers.

Tom Friedman's assertion in the *New York Times* that "we have to fight terrorists as if there are no rules" is therefore somewhat problematic for those who would apply higher religious and ethical values both to the conduct of their personal lives and to affairs of state. Judaism imposes rules even when there seem to be no rules; their application differs in degree, not in kind.

As Jews, and as Americans, we can and must retain our moral and ethical compass even as we implement unconventional rules of war. To the extent that we do so, we also will have less difficulty balancing the imperatives that drive a free society with the limitations on freedom that are necessarily imposed to maintain internal vigilance against a shadowy foe. And in achieving that balance, we will ensure that we come close to approximating a second prescription that Friedman offered in that same *New York Times* column: that we do our best to "preserve our open society as if there were no terrorists."

Dov S. Zakheim is an Under Secretary of Defense in the U.S. government.

Rules for Our Sake, Not for Our Enemies

Arnold E. Resnicoff

---

*I learned to value outrage because it reminded
me I was still human.*

I n the past, even assassins had rules. When Russian rev-
olutionaries went to bomb Grand Duke Sergei, a Czarist
official, the plan was aborted because his children were
with him. In *The Just Assassins*, Camus' play based on that
incident, one terrorist explains, "Even in destruction, there's
a right way and a wrong way — and there are limits." For
terrorists today, there's no wrong way, and no limits.

Fighting fire with fire is a natural response — but that's
what the terrorists want. They want their philosophy validated: the ends justify the means. And they want to manipu-
late our response. When terrorists linked to the National
Liberation Front in Algeria made plans to blow up a school
bus in Algeria, the French image, not French children, was
the target. And when all the non-French in the area of the
attack became immediate suspects, that served as proof for

16

the terrorist claim that racism — not "fraternity, liberty, equality" — was the value that drove French actions.

In the rivers of Vietnam, I learned to value *outrage*, because it reminded me I was still human, not yet numb to pain and horror. *Rage* was what I feared, for it could destroy the humanity I still cherished. Rage destroys our moral compass — and allows us to be manipulated by those who want us to lose our way.

Even without manipulation, it is difficult to maintain our values in the face of violence. "When you go to war," my commanding officer once said, "you fight two enemies, not one. The internal enemy is the animal within. Fight both enemies, or no one will know the players without a score-card. Fight both, or we'll remember how to fight, but not what it was that we were fighting for."

Of course, war is not the same as peace. But war and peace can never be completely separate. Either we hold on to as many values as we can or our humanity dies even if our bodies survive. Today's military values *force protection*, hoping our troops will survive the battle. But we pray that not only our bodies survive unbroken.

Former prisoners of war learned the lesson of *spiritual force protection*. Others, like Viktor Frankl, learned it in the death camps. Those who did not adapt did not last. But those who abandoned all values ultimately abandoned all hope, sometimes saving their lives at the cost of their minds — or their souls. The challenge was to avoid extremes, and — perhaps like Jacob wrestling with the angel — to struggle, to wrestle with faith and the future.

We must understand that our values are under attack because they are part of our strength. Terrorists fear our power, beginning with our image. For cynics, perception never matters — but Judaism values *maarit ayin*, how things look.

Terrorists try to destroy our values because we pose a threat to their vision of a world at war. In Beirut, I said that we Americans had the only *interfaith foxholes* in the Middle East. If the world had more interfaith foxholes, perhaps there would be less of a need altogether for foxholes.

The hard-boiled egg at the Pesach seder symbolizes our strength under pressure — the more the egg is cooked the harder it gets; the harder our times, the stronger we become. As Americans, we will find our strength during these hard times. As we pursue our response, we must maintain our outrage, acknowledging that some of our, or our enemy's, actions will never be acceptable. And we must fight the rage that distorts the importance of our own values.

Tradition teaches us that spilling drops of wine during the seder reminds us to refrain from rejoicing when our enemy suffers. We must embrace such traditions — and as Americans, we must find ways to incorporate such rituals into our lives.

A professor once told me, "Just because there are no right answers does not mean that there are no wrong answers." Exactly what the rules should be as we respond to terrorism remains unclear. But we must, at least, understand the wrong answers of both extremes: all past rules remain unchanged, and in this fight, no rules apply at all. We must fight to keep our values, not for the sake of our enemy, but for our own sake.

We must fight this war against terrorism hard and we must fight smart. But through it all, we must fight two enemies, not one. Limits must exist. And in the end we will know why we had to fight — and who we are when we come home.

Rabbi Arnold E. Resnicoff is National Director of Interreligious Affairs for The American Jewish Committee. He retired on June 1, 2001, after 28 years of active duty with the U.S. Navy. In October 1983 he was present in Beirut, Lebanon, when a suicide truck bomb attack took the lives of 241 American military personnel.

God Is in the Rubble

Michael Berenbaum

---

*The question is, what to do with the very fact
of survival.*

God had a bad week.

The killers killed in the name of God. Their religious teaching proclaimed America the great Satan and excluded Americans from an essential teaching of the Qur'an — that human beings are created in the Divine image.

We are in numb shock. How could a just God, all-powerful, all-good, and active in history permit such wanton acts of evil to take place?

Having wrestled for many years with the issue of how to speak of God and to God in the aftermath of the Holocaust, permit me some observations. Clearly, the two events are not comparable, but the study of the paradigmatic atrocity of the 20th century may shed some light on how to deal with the implications of other events.

20

Caution is required. So too, fear and trembling. Rabbi Irving Greenberg established a principle of authenticity after the Holocaust: "No statement, theological or otherwise, should be made, which cannot be made in the presence of burning children."

If we observe this principle, to call these events divine punishment — as some, like Rev. Jerry Falwell, have done — is not only to blame the victims for their own victimization, but also to blaspheme God. Surely, a benevolent God has more effective ways — less destructive ways — of instructing this nation. One post-Holocaust theologian reminded us that "history is the realm of human responsibility." The killers are responsible for their deeds.

There is a difference between tragedy and atrocity. In tragedy what we learn compensates for the price of such knowledge. Atrocity offers no such balance or compensation, and thus no inner space in which to bury the event. At most, it leaves those of us left behind searching amidst the ashes to find meaning in an event of such magnitude that it defies our very sense of meaning.

The bombing of the World Trade Center was not a tragedy but an atrocity. The capture of terrorists and the military actions in Afghanistan offer no closure to the World Trade Center and Pentagon bombings — because the justice achieved will never balance the injustice of the deed.

We are forced by the very nature of our religious traditions to ask: Where was God? If God is not to be found in the act of commission or in the choice of the victims, God is to be found amidst the rubble. If there is to be healing, God will be found amidst the ruins. Rabbi Harold Schulweis wrote of God as a "predicate." When we say God is love, we mean that loving is Godly. When we say that God is just, we also mean that doing justice is Godly.

I know that I have learned more about humanity than divinity in my study of the Holocaust. I have learned to live religiously with questions about God. I have learned to live compassionately with anguish about humanity.

It is clear to me that those who survived will suffer not only from what psychiatrists have called post-traumatic stress syndrome but what has become known as survivor guilt. In truth there is no answer. No one survived the World Trade Center or the Pentagon because of his or her virtue, strength, or wisdom. Most often, survival was random.

The question is what to do with the very fact of survival. Here, the experience of Holocaust survivors may be instructive. In the immediate days after September 11, the task of going on with life was all-consuming. Shock was eventually replaced by numbness and then depression. Because they have faced death, many survivors will have learned what is most important in life: life itself — love, family, and community.

The survivors of the World Trade Center and the Pentagon bombings will not be defined by the lives they have led until now, but the lives they will lead from now on. For the experience of near death to have ultimate meaning, it must take shape in how one rebuilds from the ashes. Such for the individual; so too, for the nation.

Michael Berenbaum, a Sh'ma *Contributing Editor, has written on the theological implications of the Holocaust. Among his 12 books is* The Holocaust: Philosophical and Religious Implications.

The Proper Blessing for Terror

Vanessa L. Ochs

Our rush to words obscures the condition we should be experiencing — a sense of horror.

On the afternoon of September 11, a Jewish student stopped by my office. The news was raw, and the feeling of being terrorized, even from afar, was one we had never rehearsed. "I feel like I should pray," she said. But she — well tutored in Jewish prayer — was blanking out, and all that came to mind, comically enough, was her bat mitzvah *haftarah* portion. I commiserated: "We're always worrying, 'what's the proper *brachah*?' In a liturgical pinch, it seems easier to be a Christian. 'Help me Jesus!' just falls into place." Going into liturgical "automatic pilot," I began leafing through the different *siddurim* and collections of new liturgies and rituals that I keep next to my desk precisely for moments when the appropriate Jewish response eludes me. There was a silence, and I rushed to fill it.

The "You've got mail" sound interrupted our conversa-

23

tion, and I saw I'd received an email from the Women of the Wall activist and scholar Rivka Haut. Assuring us her family members were okay, Haut confessed: "I want to pray. It's hard to pray now. I pray that God is watching, that God will help the trapped and injured who are yet alive, and give strength to the families of those killed. I pray that New Yorkers will come together and help each other. I pray that America will be strong and act in such a way that such acts of terrorism will never recur."

Hard as it was initially to discover the words of prayer — either words in the traditional liturgy or one's own heartfelt responses — I, like Haut, soon discovered that after the initial shock of wordlessness, any words of prayer or poetry, and any gestures of caring or remembering, turned out to be the right ones. Firemen in my town stopped cars on the road and collected money in empty boots, and that was right. Students affixed rows of roses on the walls of a tennis court, and that was the right way to create a commemorative space. I bought rolls of red ribbons for students and colleagues to tie around each other's wrists, the anti-Evil Eye ritual of my ancestors, an expression of hope for protection in a time of vulnerability, and that was right too. Whatever we said and whatever we did had the hallowed feel and power of ancient practice. Even the tasteful, understated newspaper ads placed by every company and store also felt just right — like stones placed on a national gravestone.

And now, as I write these words, the war of our vengeance has begun. Once again, I feel frozen, back to square one. What do we pray now, what do we do? On the television, I hear our leaders offering statements that sound nearly liturgical: "We are a united front. We have the complete cooperation of our friends." And there are the goodly gestures: "We will help the people of Afghanistan, we will drop food." I picture people looking up, wondering if the bundle hurtling toward them is a bomb or a box of Rice Krispies.

Like Haut, I feel compelled to continue searching for words of prayer and gestures that pull us out of the stupor of our shock and fear. Probably tomorrow, some group will ask me to say a prayer or recite another Yehuda Amichai poem at a vigil, to offer some meaning-making words or gestures that come out of Jewish tradition. I anticipate that once again students will come to my office, and they will say that life has lost its meaning and they are not sure of the point of going on.

As a mother who has kissed many boo-boos, I go automatically into soothing mode. But I am beginning to feel that rushing to pray, and rushing to find gestures of repair and loving-kindness, are the too-quick fixes we turn to because we need them to obscure what is indeed the condition we should be experiencing — a sense of horror. That horror should not be so easily remedied. There are times when we truly need to endure meaninglessness. At times like this, it should be very, very hard to pray.

Vanessa L. Ochs, a Sh'ma *Contributing Editor, is the Ida and Nathan Kolodiz Director of Jewish Studies at the University of Virginia in Charlottesville.*

Prayer in Response to Terror

William H. Lebeau

Prayer is a natural response to horror.

On the morning of September 11, I gathered with a stunned community of students, faculty, and staff at the Jewish Theological Seminary. Of many different faiths, colors, and ethnic and national backgrounds, never did we feel more unified, desperately needing one another for solace. Assembling for prayer was a natural step, which we took confident we would find universal words of entreaty to God. Asked to lead an ecumenical service, I chose as the central text Psalm 94. It asks God to bring just retribution upon the perpetrators of evil, reflecting our collective rage; its spirit, I hoped, would ultimately motivate us to act against forces that threatened to enervate us at a time when we could not afford to let our resolve slip.

Prayer, a natural response to tragedy, stands at the heart of every faith community. Its language embodies the foundational texts, collective experience, needs, and aspirations of each religion's adherents. Even individuals without formal religious affiliation, therefore, turn to prayer to express intense feelings of joy, adversity, or vulnerability that surpass the human capacity to grasp the full understanding of life's experiences.

Is it any wonder then, that, as the steel and concrete of the World Trade Center crumbled into rubble and ashes, prayers proliferated. We prayed for our country and for our leaders; we even blessed each other in casual conversations. *God Bless America* became the anthem of choice, allowing us to pray that God's "light from above" guide us through our dark night of national tragedy. People flocked to houses of worship in search of comfort. We were fearful of an emotional paralysis threatening to overtake us in a world spinning out of control.

What is embedded in the liturgy that makes it so compelling? Jewish tradition provides keen insight into the role of prayer in the human experience. In Genesis, for example, we read of Noah, who, as the floodwaters receded, constructed an altar to declare his overwhelming feelings of gratitude to God for sparing his life. Pained by barrenness, ancient matriarchs and patriarchs prayed for children. Moses petitioned God to heal Miriam's leprosy. David gave prayerful voice to emotions of triumph, despair, and hope through the poetry of his Psalms.

The *siddur*, historically a unifying force in shaping the experience of prayer for the Jewish community, serves as a template for incorporating prayer into our lives today. It enables us to filter the harsh, often conflicting realities we confront into segments fraught with universal meaning.

Through its set order of prayer and the fixed regimen of daily worship, Jews male and female, of every age and level of education, approach God with one voice. Yet in that shared encounter, each individual can access the deepest recesses of humanity and explore his or her unique connection to God in a search for meaning. Perhaps, therefore, the most critical message of the siddur is this simple one: that prayer is not meant to be reserved for extraordinary, urgent moments, but its power, rather, is to be found in the daily, monthly, and yearly cycles of prayer we are commanded to repeat. And that, if we adhere to the laws of worship, God will never long be far from our grasp.

And so on the day of the tragic attacks, we recited the passionate words *"Kel n'kamot HaShem Kel n'kamot hofee-a. Hee-na-say Shofet ha-aretz hashev g'mul al ge-im ad matai r'sha'im HaShem, ad matai r'shaim ya-a-lozu?"* Lord, God of retribution appear. Arise, Judge of the earth and take recompense upon the arrogant. How long O Lord shall the wicked rejoice? (Psalm 94)

Abraham Joshua Heschel (z"l), in *Quest for God*, taught that we say these words of prayer, "not to change God, but to change ourselves." We say them to steel ourselves against the inclination to abandon our responsibility for repair of the world. In our frustration we cry out to God to unleash Divine fury on the perpetrators of evil and right human failings. We have been to that place before with God on many other terrible days in human history. We have been ready to be relieved of our burden of world affairs. In frustration we have been willing to succumb to control by the Divine Hand, if only human conflict could be eliminated.

But biblical, rabbinic, and liturgical sources instruct that the Almighty has another plan for humanity. God endowed us with the privilege of determining human destiny. Psalm 94 must be prayed as if we are willing to give everything over to God. However, its real power lies in its ability to transform us and inspire us to accept the responsibility to hear God urging us, *tzedek tzedek tirdof* — pursue justice; marshal the forces of humanity; pursue and root out those who would arrogantly destroy life.

In Tractate Menahot 43b, Rabbi Meir reveals the essence of Jewish prayer. He taught, "*Hayav adam l'varekh meah b'rakhot b'khol yom*" — A person is obligated to recite 100 blessings every day. Our morning prayers bless God for the gifts of our bodies, our souls, sight, breath, freedom of movement, sunrise and sunset — blessings that remain even when adversity strikes. Rabbi Meir understood that by the conclusion of the daily recitation, we achieve the perspective necessary to sustain our faith in life's beauty and ultimate meaning.

At least for a precious moment in time following the attacks of September 11, as prayers proliferated, millions of human beings were uttering 100 *b'rakhot* each day. We counted the members of our families and were thankful for those unharmed. Collectively, our prayers changed us. We performed godly acts of genuine courage, kindness, and sensitivity. Prejudice, if only briefly, seemed to disappear.

We need Rabbi Meir's certainty that prayer, even on more ordinary days, helps us to maximize our potential. It can transform the godly sparks within each of us into raging fires of passion to repair the world so we come to resemble the humans that God intended when we were brought into being. Unquestionably, prayer offers an inherently powerful response to tragedy. But that response, Judaism makes clear, is most effective when it derives from its own foundation of strength — an ongoing active participation in its daily call.

_____

Rabbi William H. Lebeau is Vice Chancellor for Rabbinic Development at the Jewish Theological Seminary of America.

Rethinking Liberty in the Age of Terrorism

Alan M. Dershowitz

It is far better for everybody to be deprived of a little bit of anonymity than for one specific ethnic group to bear a disproportionate part of the burden.

The transforming events of September 11, and since, have led many thoughtful people to rethink and reassess some of their most fundamental values. That is as it should be, since values — like rights — grow out of experience. History has shown us that everything changes with experience, including religion, constitutional interpretation, and moral values. The Holocaust changed theology. The Civil War altered concepts of equality. And the terrorist attacks of September 11 have changed the way many people think about good and evil.

A case in point: In the years preceding the terrorists' attack on the World Trade Center, I would present my students with a classroom hypothetical very close to the facts of September 11 and ask them whether it would be proper to shoot down a passenger jet about to crash into an occupied building. There was considerable debate about this "hypo-thetical," with many religious students espousing the view that it is always wrong to kill innocent people intentionally, even if these people had only moments to live and killing them would save the lives of other innocent people. Theological and philosophical arguments were invoked on both sides, and the debate was always lively. The events of September 11 ended that debate forever. Having experienced the catastrophe resulting from the passenger jets being used as airborne missiles, every reasonable and thoughtful person now believes that shooting down the passenger jet would be the only appropriate response. Theologians and philoso-phers are scurrying around trying to conform their preexist-ing doctrines to the conclusion they know is now required if they are to be taken seriously in the future. Now that we know the right answer, we must figure out how to frame the question in order to assure that we get that answer.

The same can be said about liberties. Many thoughtful lib-ertarians are now rethinking their knee-jerk opposition to some new technologies that may assist us in fighting terror-ism. I must admit that I am one of those who are rethinking some of my previously held views. For example, when I first heard about roving wiretaps — which follow a specific per-son rather than a specific telephone — I was immediately suspicious. My suspicions arose in part because these taps were used primarily in the so-called war against drugs — a war that I do not believe is worthy of any rethinking of civil libertarian values. Now that I understand that the roving wiretap can play an important role in tracking potential ter-rorists who use cell phones briefly and then discard and replace them, I have begun to think hard about whether there

are any real down sides to a roving warrant. I have concluded that there are not. Indeed, it is far better to focus a search
on a specific person against whom a warrant has been
obtained based on probable cause than on a specific telephone that might easily be used by innocent people. The
Supreme Court has said that the Fourth Amendment "pro-
tects people, not places." It would seem to follow that a warrant directed at a person, rather than a telephone or a place,
would serve the privacy interests protected by that amendment.

The events of September 11 have also prompted me to
rethink my previous opposition to national identity cards.
My opposition to these cards grew primarily out of the mis-
use of such cards by the apartheid regime in South Africa and
the totalitarian regimes in the Soviet Union and China. But
the ease with which several of the September 11 hijackers
managed to hide in open view and fall between the bureau-
cratic cracks made it clear to me that a foolproof national ID
card had some real virtues. Then I started to think about its
vices. I was hard-pressed to come up with any compelling
civil libertarian arguments against a simple card that would
contain only five elements: the bearer's name, address, Social
Security number, photograph, and a finger or retinal print
matching a chip in the card. This chip would make it virtually impossible for anyone to use a card that was not his or
hers, and would allow appropriate authorities under appropriate circumstances to check the identity of all people prop-
erly in this country.

There are, of course, grave dangers inherent in any system
of information gathering by government officials. Anyone
who lived through J. Edgar Hoover's tenure as the director of

the FBI understands this danger. There should be a national debate over what kind of information is appropriate for the government to gather and place in its databases. But that is a different debate than the one about national identity cards. The debate about ID cards should be a stimulus to the far more important debates about the content of government databases and the circumstances under which government authorities should be entitled to ask anyone to identify him- or herself.

Another virtue of the national ID card is that it would eliminate much of the justification now offered for racial or ethnic profiling. I have some experience to back that up. When African-American students first started to attend Harvard in significant numbers, many of them were routinely hassled by security officers and others, since they didn't "look" as if they "belonged" on or around the Harvard campus. When ID cards were issued to all students, it became far easier for the African-American students to avoid harassment by simply showing their cards. To be sure, African-American students were asked to show their cards more often than white students — and that clearly is inappropriate. But the net result of the ID cards was to reduce the amount of inappropriate hassling of minority students. I think the same thing would be true for Arab-Americans. Under current conditions, Arab-American men would probably be asked for their IDs more often, but by showing the card, they could avoid the kind of harassment that many have recently experienced on airplanes.

As a general proposition, I think it is far better for everybody to be deprived of a little bit of anonymity than for one specific ethnic group to bear a disproportionate part of the burden. Those people who deliberately opt out of the national ID system have made a decision to endure more intrusive searches in exchange for not having to carry the card. In some respects, this is a little like the trade-off people make when they agree to have their automobile identified by a radio computer when crossing bridges and going through tunnels, rather than stopping and paying an anonymous toll.

Terrorists should never make us give up our liberties or change our values. But experiences of all kinds — whether they are natural disasters or the horrors wrought by criminals — inevitably provoke thoughtful people into rethinking attitudes and values. This process is a healthy one. It is part of what Socrates called "the examined life."

Alan M. Dershowitz is Professor of Law at Harvard University. His most recent book is Shouting Fire: Civil Liberties in a Turbulent Age, *published by Little, Brown.*

Understanding the Power of Words of War

Dawn Rose

We are given the message that peacetime rules, of necessity, must be suspended.

"THE evil ones have declared war on us and our way of life. They hate freedom and democracy. We're going to smoke 'em out of their caves." The White House's verbal portrait of the events of September 11 has been frightfully effective, resulting in a quick and positive response from Congress and the American people.

Judaism has long understood the potency of the spoken word. With words, we construct meaning; we make sense of the universe — from passive permission to active enablement.

Because the United States requires public support for what it is doing both here and in Afghanistan, any inquiry into the ethics of a global manhunt from a Jewish perspective must begin by understanding the impact of these words of war and the near-universal acclaim they have garnered.

36

Politics, even or especially the politics of war, is very much about selling images and ideas. A fundamental principle guides Jewish ethics in this area: "*Lifnei ha-iver, lo titen mikshol.*" — Put no stumbling block before the blind." (Leviticus 19:14) Interpreted as a sweeping prohibition against using the public's ignorance against itself, this tenet forbids the use of misleading advertising or sales techniques that prey upon people's desires, fears, insecurities, and most significantly, lack of knowledge or information.

It is here that the Bush administration has been so bold — in the language with which it has sold this war. The first selling point is that it is, in fact, a war. Within the *weltanschauung* introduced with this word, it is logical and appropriate that the full weight of the military be engaged; "peripheral" issues — social and economic — be tabled; and global alliances be demanded. With war there is always an enemy who must be evil even as we are good. War, however complicated, demands this simplicity, without which we cannot kill with impunity. More, this is a "new" war, the likes of which we have never seen before. Right away the message is that peacetime rules, of necessity, must be suspended. And, with the adjective "new" we learn that the rules developed through painful past history about human rights during wartime might not apply.

President Bush has declared that freedom and democracy are under attack by those who "hate our way of life." The emotional associations those words elicit obfuscate the impossibly abstract nature of the assertion. Millions of Americans stand, flag in hand, never thinking to ask the most basic and obvious questions: Which freedoms? For whom? What about our way of life could possibly affect distant cultures and economies so adversely?

With these presidential words — these simplified concepts of hatred — every American feels attacked. With these words, no one is offered appropriate information about the roots of the conflict or the nature of the struggle. Yet Americans are supporting this war, sending our sons and daughters, and promising billions of dollars in funds. Tirelessly, the Administration and the media inundate Americans with visual images that proclaim: To do less is to sully the muddy graves of the World Trade Center victims; to do less is to ignore with cowardice this danger to our homeland.

Perhaps the most shameful line the Administration has generated is "This is not a war against the Afghan people." We know that civilian Afghans will bear the brunt of the war. We are patiently told to learn the difference between *intended* loss of civilian life (the WTC) and "unintended" (though anticipated) loss of civilian life (Afghanistan).

Certainly Judaism has long recognized distinctions between accidental and intentional injury and death. However, these distinctions apply to legal responsibility *after the fact*. *Before the act*, the Administration announced its decision to proceed on a course that, of practical necessity, incurs unintended loss of innocent life.

We have been told that we are "at war," and the implication is made that innocent lives are thus expendable — especially of those people who are not American, not Jewish or Christian, and not the family down the block. We must demand that President Bush call death, death — whether it occurs at home or abroad. We must educate ourselves against the inundating media spin. Only then do we have a chance to discover what our rock-bottom ethical questions are in this crisis and begin to address them appropriately.

Dawn Rose holds a Ph.D. in Jewish Philosophy from the Jewish Theological Seminary. She is currently Rabbinic Leader of the Temple of Universal Judaism in New York City, a community founded on the principles of interfaith outreach and dialogue.

A Light Unto the Nation: Sharing a Jewish Ethic with America

Irving "Yitz" Greenberg

The hard lessons learned from Jewish history should be shared with Americans: Evil must be confronted thoroughly and with force sufficient to defeat it.

The catastrophe inflicted by terrorists on September 11 has driven home a fundamental moral lesson of the Holocaust — the ethical centrality of power.

The incredible expansion of power (military, scientific, and economic) in contemporary life has broken the balance of power between aggressors and victims. Unlimited oppression is now possible. We must, therefore, amass sufficient power for potential victims to defend themselves successfully.

This is a moral revolution: the only serious moral code is an ethic of power — how, when, and why to exercise force. The shift can be described simply: One gives up purity and innocence — for power is corrupting — in return for effectiveness in upholding the highest value, life.

Jewry must explain this revolution to America. Practicing

40

an ethic of powerlessness in the face of all-powerful evil constitutes abdication of moral responsibility. It may even constitute collaboration with evil, for as the Talmud says, "One who shows mercy to those [evil people] who deserve harshness [to stop them] will end up showing harshness [allowing evil to attack] to those [good people] who deserve mercy."

As the attack on the Twin Towers shows, the perpetrators will use force without limit against civilians and innocents, seeking to maximize the loss of life in order to terrorize people into submission. The bioterrorism scare reflects the recognition that if the radicals could, they would kill hundreds of thousands, even millions. This threat can only be addressed by the use of force and a universal hunt for the terrorists until they are stopped. Holding back because of anti-war sentiments or letting monetary considerations dominate — such as the scrimping on airline security — constitutes a cheapening of life.

An ethic of power binds two poles — the ideal and the real — in dynamic interaction. The classic Jewish goal of life's triumph is the ethical standard. The ethical principle is that force is never self-justifying; it must operate in service of the good, indeed, of the highest good. This gives primacy to life-saving (*pikuach nefesh*), especially by establishing a world that respects the infinite value, equality, and uniqueness of every human being.

The ethical tension begins with our imperfect world, where evil forces operate. Defensive war is morally necessary to stop evil and prevent mass murder. The guiding principle is to use no more power than necessary, to give priority for lifesaving, and to minimize civilian casualties. This even includes taking some casualties of one's own to avoid indiscriminate slaughter.

The Bush Administration is gearing up for war, but many Americans hesitate or recoil from new ethical dilemmas. American Jews can help by sharing the hard-earned lessons of Jewish life in the past half-century, especially experiences drawn from life in Israel. These lessons would include the following:

1) Evil must be confronted thoroughly and with force sufficient to defeat it. To appease is shortsighted and, as the September 11 events show, futile. Similarly, establishing a coalition in which terror-sponsoring states can join with no significant change of behavior could preserve terrorism to strike another day, could be read as a signal that there is no cost for harboring terror, and could discourage moderate Islamists from making the needed but excruciatingly difficult choice to go with a Western/humanist orientation over the drive toward radicalization.

2) The best, most realistic ethical options should be articulated, drawing on Israel's hard-earned moral model: (a) However painful, preventive assassination of terrorist leaders is preferable to mass attacks and population transfers otherwise needed to quell terror. (b) Reducing legal loopholes and using controlled force (but not torture) to procure needed information on imminent attacks from detained terrorists is acceptable. (c) Responsible censorship and voluntary limits on the flow of information for security purposes should not cripple free media or override the functioning of multiple (opposition) political parties. (d) Generic stereotyping of Arabs should be avoided and distinctions between Islamic followers acknowledged, while using legitimate profiling as one tool to prevent terrorist attacks.

The September 11 attacks ended the period when U.S. Jews could imagine that they would live in peace, safely with their children, while Israel twisted in the winds of terror and the violent Intifada alone. Recognizing that danger is universal, the correct response is to intensify travel and social/educational links to Israel — to share fate and comfort, and learn from each other.

Similarly, American Jews must explain why the need to form a coalition should not lead to pressuring Israel to make concessions without cessation of the Intifada/violence. Such a reward for terrorism would rebound to hurt America. It will take inner courage and identification with Jewish destiny for American Jews not to be tempted into silence or distance themselves from Israel when Bin Laden's false claims that America is being attacked because it is allied with Israel are voiced. Standing up will be the expression of the unity of Jewish people and its shared fate. Ironically, I believe that it might ultimately reopen a serious possibility of a negotiated peace for Israel.

Rabbi Irving "Yitz" Greenberg is President of the Jewish Life Network. Author of The Jewish Way, *he has written extensively on post-Holocaust theology, the ethics of power, and pluralism.*

Learning and Teaching

Helping Children Cope with a Violent World

Sheryl H. Katz and Maxine Segal Handelman

Judaism supports our children by providing rituals and actions that help them see that challenges can be met with a commitment to good.

In the world of America before September 11, 2001, we could pretend that the children we care for could live in a perfect world without fear, violence, or scary things. With a false sense of our own invulnerability, we could pretend that living under the constant threat of terrorism and violence existed somewhere else and happened to other people.

In truth, today our youngest children are exposed to many frightening images and words as part of their daily lives. American children watch an average of four hours of TV a day, 28 hours a week, 2,400 hours a year, with prime hours occurring before dinner. When tragedies occur, the repetition of images on TV increases the likelihood that children will hear or see something disturbing. With the current state of the world, exposure to violent images and words about death and loss needs to be monitored. How each child is affected by these events, and how he or she will react, depends upon the child's age, past experience, and current level of stress.

As teachers and parents, we need to give children the opportunity to talk about their reactions to disturbing world events. For children under the age of three, all that may be necessary is to reaffirm our love by providing increased warmth, rocking, and the knowledge that we are available. For older children, we must reassure them that adults at home and at school know how to take care of them and keep them safe.

We improve our children's ability to cope with stress by helping them acknowledge a sense of control over the situation, view change as a challenge, and feel a commitment to clear values. Proactively, parents can let children know that it is okay to talk about what they have heard in the media or from friends. During a major news event, you might raise a general question, such as "What have you heard about ... ?" and allow a long pause for answers (try counting to 75). Let each child speak, and record the responses. Writing down children's words gives them a sense of control. Children understand information differently than adults, so first find out what they do and do not understand. Don't jump to conclusions and provide too much information. Listen, reflect their emotions, and reassure them that you know this is frightening and that the adults are doing all that must be done to make things safer.

Answer questions by following their lead and giving small pieces of information. Watch how the children react before going further. Children personalize the scary things they hear. Reassure them about their own safety: "This won't happen to you, because your parents and teachers are doing everything to keep you safe." Rabbi David Wolpe offers further insights in his book *Teaching Children About God*: "A way to bring God into the picture is to remind children that God gave us the gift of being able to make choices. Some people make choices that hurt or sadden others. The consequences of free will granted by God may seem unfair to children and adults." Discuss how Judaism helps us to know how to make good choices about helping others in need, *tzedakah*, and fixing the places that have been damaged, *tikkun olam*. Remind children about the actions of care givers, *gemilut hasadim*, like doctors, firefighters, and police officers. Knowledge of and commitment to values like these help children become stronger in the face of adversity.

When children report specific worries, ask them to dictate a story or draw a picture. Listen. Observe their play to get a sense of how they are understanding and working through what they have heard. Children master stressful feelings through repetitive play with puppets, figures, and other toys. Roleplaying allows children to see that strong feelings can be managed safely. Find opportunities to point out positive, nonviolent ways in which children solve their own problems. Tell them, "I get upset when people solve their problems by hurting each other. Remember when you were angry with Susie for... ? You used your words." Point out the acts of *chesed*, kindness.

Judaism gives us many avenues to be proactive in the face of tragedy. Seek out community worship and memorial opportunities that you can share with your child. Fulfill the mitzvah of *bikkur holim*, visiting the sick, by creating get-well cards with your child and sending them to the injured, or by calling friends and relatives in the affected areas. Fulfill the mitzvah of *pikuah nefesh*, saving a life, by donating blood. Explain to your child why you are doing this. Light a *yizkor* candle in your home. Write a prayer with your child and offer it as a family around the dinner table. Provide opportunities for your child to write letters to those amidst the struggle in Israel or Afghanistan.

The beliefs of our faith support our children by providing rituals and actions that help them see that challenges can be met with a commitment to good. To help our children handle these stresses, we need to provide a predictable environment that models and teaches conflict resolution skills, demonstrates kindness and nurturing in our interactions with others, and allows children to share their feelings. Most of all, we need to listen.

Sheryl H. Katz is Director of Social Services, Early Childhood, JCCs of Chicago, and former Chairperson of Early Childhood Education at Montay College.

Maxine Segal Handelman is Director of Early Childhood Jewish Education, Pritzker Center, JCCs of Chicago. She is the author of Jewish Every Day.

Based upon: "Media Violence and Young Children" from the National Association for the Education of Young Children, copyright 1997 by NAEYC. "Violence and Young Children's Development" ERIC Digest. "Discussing the News with 3 to 7 year olds; What to Do?" Sydney Gurewitz Clemens, c. 2000, NAEYC. Childhood Stress, 1987 by Barbara Kuczen, "Immediate Response Curriculum September 11, 2001: A Day of National Tragedy," Jewish Education Center of Cleveland.

Looking Within: Reading Sacred Violent Texts

Michael Balinsky

---

*Working with troubling texts forces us to
acknowledge the violence within our own
sacred writings and approach the writings of
other religions with more sensitivity.*

The horrible acts of September 11 have raised questions
about how a religious tradition reads its sacred texts
that define the "other" and sanctions violence against
them. As many have begun to look at texts of violence in the
Qur'an, it becomes imperative for the Jewish community to
begin investigating its own sacred texts of violence.
Strategies employed in reading texts that advocate violence
against the "other" cut across religious lines. It is hoped that
through this session participants will gain knowledge of how
Jews have addressed these concerns and enable them to participate with a critical eye in interreligious discussion.

This session builds on the work of others and while it
makes no claim of offering original ideas, it is the sequencing
of these ideas and their application to the current situation
that brings something new to our discussion. Rather than

simply giving information, it is structured on the idea that quality adult learning can emerge from an honest engagement with Jewish text in an interactive environment.

The following journals have been used in preparation. It is strongly recommended that the leader of the session read these in advance. Both are available on the Internet.

Textual Reasoning, Volume 8, 1999
(www.bu.edu/mzank/Textual_Reasoning/general.html)
Sh'ma: A Journal of Jewish Responsibility
April 2001 (www.shma.com)

Goal: The specific intent of this session is to have participants wrestle with these texts of violence and to see the strategy of reading participants employ. In doing so, they will also have to see how their strategy meshes with their understanding of the sacred nature and authority of Torah. They will develop a critical eye in analyzing the strategies employed by the selected commentaries.

Format: This session is structured as an interactive experience in which student participation is central. The leader should help the participants formulate their positions, clarify questions, and provide additional material and background, but this session will work best if the students' voices play the key role.

Questions are provided with the texts. The texts themselves should provoke much discussion. In discussing their reactions to the texts, students should be encouraged to take the second step to see how their understanding relates to their conception of Torah. What should emerge is a variety of strategies and positions. Shaul Magid, in *Textual*

Reasoning, lists three of many approaches: (1) de-Judaizing the text; (2) allegorizing the text; and (3) reading the text against itself (for examples, see his article). Other approaches may include confining the violent event to a particular historical era, which from either a (4) technical legal point (Canaanites no longer exist today) or an (5) ethical understanding, makes the law sanctioning violence no longer applicable; (6) suggesting that the event is not historical at all, but is being used by the biblical a(A)uthor to formulate a central religious position. It will be helpful to list these and refer back to them.

It is particularly important, as the discussion can get quite heated, that disagreements be framed within the broader picture of the participants' assumptions about the nature of Torah and the implications that emerge out of it. Depending on one's understanding of Torah, not all approaches may be found acceptable.

The session is divided into two parts: biblical texts and commentary. It is suggested that following an introduction, the three biblical texts be read, with minimal comments made by the leader except to elaborate on their context within the Torah, and followed by time for discussion. This discussion is the core piece of the session. After listing strategies, the commentaries should be read to see what strategy they employ, their understanding of the authority of Torah, and any additional discussion they provoke.

It is most likely that the two parts will take from one to two hours.

Reading Sacred Violent Texts

1. Provide texts for Numbers 31:1-16 (the war with the Midianites), Deuteronomy 20:9-18 (the war with the seven

nations), and Deuteronomy 25:17-19 (the war with Amalek). These excerpts from the Torah mandate extreme violence and war against certain enemies of the Jewish people. As these are from the Torah, and are read in congregations as part of the weekly Torah reading, they are viewed as much more than "historical" texts, but are part of that which we deem sacred. How do we read these texts today? What strategies can we employ in reading these troubling texts?

2. The examples below, the first classical and the second contemporary, address the authority and interpretation of the Torah sources. What strategy does each employ? How do you react to their approaches?

(A) Maimonides, *Laws of Kings and Their Wars* 5:4, writes the following regarding the seven nations of Canaan:
> It is a positive commandment to destroy the seven nations, as it is said: "But thou shall utterly destroy them" (Deuteronomy 20:17). If one does not kill any of them that falls into one's power, one transgresses a negative commandment, as it is said: "Thou shall save nothing that breathes" (Deuteronomy 20:16). But their memory [their identity] has long since perished."

(B) "How Liberal Jews Read the Torah," by Robert M. Seltzer (excerpted from *Torat Hayyim* — Union of American Hebrew Congregations):

> This week's double *parashah, Matot/Mas'ei*, contains one of the most problematic stories in the Pentateuch. Encamped not far from Jericho, across the Jordan River

in the land of Moab, the Israelites take up arms against the Midianites. They slaughter all the males and under Moses' direction, kill their women and children, with the exception of "every young woman who has not had carnal relations with a man." (Numbers 31:18) The question arises, How could God have ordered such a massacre?

... This is hardly our liberal understanding of the spirit of the Torah as embodied in "Do not murder," "Love your neighbor as yourself," and "Justice, justice shall you pursue." Over the course of Jewish history, more universal, broad-minded, and compassionate values were increasingly used to reinterpret and in effect to abolish injunctions that were narrowly retributive.

As exponents of liberal Judaism, we don't have to rationalize on religious grounds the mass slaughter of any enemy. Religious fanaticism is a manifestation of the *yetzer hara*, "bad instinct," and not the *yetzer hatov*, "instinct to do good." For Isaiah, the goal of history was the abolition of war and the end of violence on earth. Most of us accept that killing in self-defense is at times unavoidable, but only under severe duress and against combatants and blatant murderers, never for revenge.

Should we therefore regret that this story is included in the Pentateuch? Is the Torah in the broad, comprehensive sense lessened by it? No. This tale may indeed reflect the setting in which ethical monotheism germinated. Liberal Jews are not fundamentalists in the sense that everything in the Torah has to be morally justified. There are simply some passages that can only be understood historically, as an expression of passions that humanity has had to struggle to overcome and still does. Confronting this tale links us obscurely to the very beginnings of the Jewish heritage, when it had to confront an inhospitable and threatening world, but physical and religious survival require of us much more discriminating means of self-defense that are respectful of the essential humanity of the foe. The lesson is that we read this story in order to remember to forget it.

Conclusion

In the Prologue to his book *Studies in the Bible and Jewish Thought* (JPS 1995), Moshe Greenberg lists three qualities (in addition to academic and critical skills) that are necessary for Jewish Bible scholarship.

1. Humility — that is, an openness to the new and the innovative, and to continuing debate that entails modesty and lack of dogmatism.

2. Respect for the text — expressed in a systematic search for its "truth," in the universal-human sense as well as the particularistically Jewish; for the wealth of meanings contained in it; and for its art of expression.

3. A sense of responsibility toward a community whose members await disclosure of the scriptural message.

These three qualities of humility, respect, and responsibility can inform nonacademic adult learners as well. As they struggle with violence to the "other" in Jewish tradition, and the tension between a search for truth and understanding with a sense of responsibility to the Torah and their fellow Jews, they should come to realize that many Muslims and Christians engage their sacred violent texts with the same tension. We have the right to demand an investigation of these texts and the ideology expressed therein, but we can do so only in light of our struggles with our own sacred texts.

Rabbi Michael Balinsky is Director of Faculty Development for the Florence Melton Adult Mini-Schools and author of "Preparing to Teach: The Florence Melton Adult Mini-School Faculty Handbook." Before joining the FMAMS, Rabbi Balinsky was Hillel Director of the Louis and Saerree Fiedler Hillel Center at Northwestern University for 19 years. Rabbi Balinsky is a past president of the Chicago Board of Rabbis and has served on the boards of the Jewish Federation of Metropolitan Chicago and the American Jewish Committee. A graduate of Yeshiva University, he is married to Dr. Myra Rapoport and father of three daughters. If you would like additional commentaries that may be taught with this material, please write to mbalinsky@fmams.org.il.

Ritual, Text, and Creativity: Responding to World Tragedy in a Pluralistic Jewish Day School Setting

Or Rose

As a Jewish educator, I feel blessed to have a rich and varied storehouse of rituals, prayers, ideas, and texts to draw upon during times of pain and confusion.

September 11, 2001, started like most other days at Boston's Jewish Community Day School — students poured out of the big yellow buses, parents ushered their children into the building before rushing off to work, and teachers milled about making last-minute preparations before their classes. No one could have imagined that by 9:30 our world would be changed forever.

As word of the terrorist attacks reached the school, faculty members gathered in the school office and quickly formulated response strategies. The decision was made to share the news with the children one class at a time, so as not to overwhelm them. In our initial conversations with the children we attempted to share what little information we had available to us in a calm and straightforward manner. Drawing on the wisdom of the Jewish tradition, when words failed us, we turned to song and prayer. The Book of Psalms was the obvious choice, as Jews have turned to this ancient collection of poetry for comfort and guidance for thousands of years.

On the morning following the attacks, we held a special schoolwide *Shaharit* (morning prayer) service during which memorial candles were lit, selections from *Tehilim* (Psalms) were recited, and students and faculty read selected English and Hebrew poetry. Although we pray every morning at JCDS, on September 12 the intensity of the service was unlike anything I have experienced with my students — the familiar words of the *siddur* (prayer book) were infused with a new sense of urgency and intention.

Over the course of the next several days, students were given the opportunity to continue discussing the current events in their classes and individually with their *madrichim*, or faculty mentors. The school psychologist also made herself available for conversation with faculty, students, and families.

Ironically, in the days before the terrorist attacks, the faculty decided that one of this year's educational foci in our middle school would be "diversity and tolerance." Sadly, we did not have to turn to history books for educational materials; our day-to-day lives provided more material than any of us could have ever wanted.

One of the central frameworks for our work on diversity and tolerance has been the middle school *Beit Midrash*. Traditionally, a *beit midrash* is a study house where Jewish students gather to explore religious texts. Building on this model, the JCDS *Beit Midrash* program combines tradition and innovation. Our program is interdisciplinary — texts are drawn from a range of Jewish and non-Jewish sources and teachers from different disciplines plan and facilitate these sessions. Significant time is devoted to *hevrutah* (peer) learning and group discussion. As a complement to their studies, students also participate in a variety of creative workshops — including drama, music, and the visual arts — as well as social action programs.

Given the timing of the terrorist attacks, we attempted to tease apart the strands of this complicated situation through an examination of several High Holiday texts and rituals. In one session, for example, we looked at a number of liturgical selections that speak of Rosh Hashanah as a time of judgment — a time when God evaluates human behavior and decides who will live and who will die. Needless to say, the events of September 11 forced us to rethink what these texts teach us. What was God's role in the attacks? Why did so many innocent people die in New York, Washington, and Pennsylvania? Should our Rosh Hashanah prayers be amended in any way this year? As a pluralistic institution, we do not provide any one answer to such difficult theological questions; rather we present our students with a number of different possibilities from the canon of Jewish thought — the Talmud, Maimonides, the Ba'al Shem Tov, and Nehama Leibowitz. What we do attempt to convey to them is that there is a range of authentic Jewish responses to any issue, including ones that no previous scholar or sage has articulated — responses that only they can create or discover.

In our next session, we turned our attention to *tashlich* — a High Holiday ritual in which we symbolically cast off our sins by throwing breadcrumbs into a body of water. One of the texts used in this ceremony is taken from the biblical book of Micah (7:18-20). This passage proclaims, like many others in the Torah, that God is "compassionate, forgiving the iniquities of His people." In this case we focused our attention not on God, but on *our own* capacity for forgiveness after September 11. Could we, should we, forgive the suicide attackers? Is there a difference between forgiving and forgetting? What separates justice from revenge? In this context, we also discussed the power of the Jewish calendar, which serves as a vital framework in which to sanctify and celebrate the tapestry of human life.

As the cycle of fall holidays passed, we began an exploration of Islamic culture and religion. One of the messages of September 11 that we wanted to convey to our students was the importance of understanding the rich and multi-dimensional nature of this ancient tradition. As Jews, we felt a particular responsibility to explore this subject given the long and complex relationship of these two Abrahamic faiths. In one difficult but important exercise, we read selections from the Qur'an (Islamic scripture) and the *TaNaKh* (the Hebrew Bible) and found that both sacred texts contain messages of love and hatred for people of other faiths and backgrounds. This led us to an impassioned discussion about the uses and abuses of religious teachings and the power of the interpreter to shape his or her reality.

The terrifying events of September 11 have left us all thinking, questioning, and searching for meaning. As educators, we are faced with the challenge of trying to make meaning in our lives and to help our students make meaning in their lives. As a Jewish educator, I feel blessed to have a rich and varied storehouse of rituals, prayers, ideas, and texts to draw upon during times of pain and confusion. These resources serve as powerful tools with which to engage my students in matters of ultimate concern.

Or Rose is a Judaic studies teacher at the Jewish Community Day School in Newton, MA, and a Ph.D. student in Jewish Thought at Brandeis University in Waltham, MA. The Jewish Community Day School is a nondenominational educational institution for Jewish students ages 5 to 14 (K-8th grade).

A Lesson Plan on Fighting Terrorism: Jewish Views on Warfare

David Elcott

Children are taught the differences between milhemet mitzvah *(an obligatory war) and* milhemet reshut *(a discretionary war).*

In this lesson, students will study texts that form the foundation of Jewish attitudes toward war. Through their investigation students will distinguish between a *milhemet mitzvah* (an obligatory or commanded war) and a *milhemet reshut* (a discretionary war).

Concepts and Objectives
Rabbinic tradition defines two different types of war and the obligations for each.

War is considered a mitzvah under certain circumstances.

Motivation and Development
1. Distribute copies of the three-column chart illustrated on the next page.

	Milhemet Mitzvah	*Milhemet Reshut*
Translation		
Objective(s) of the war	1.	1.
	2.	
	3.	
Who declares the war?		
Who is exempt from fighting?		
Example (Historical)		
Example (Contemporary)		

2. Study the texts that address the question of war in Jewish tradition. As you define an element of war, place it in the appropriate spot on the chart.

3. To conclude the lesson, ask students to give examples of a *milhemet mitzvah* and a *milhemet reshut*, based on their knowledge of history and current events.

Does everyone agree with the examples?

Can we always know the difference? Why or why not?

Jewish Texts
Maimonides, Mishneh Torah, Hilkhot Melakhim 5:1-2

"A king does not initiate war except in a *milhemet mitzvah*. What is a *milhemet mitzvah*? A war on the seven nations [inhabiting Canaan], a war on the Amalekites, and [a war] to assist Jews from a danger that threatens them. Other than this is a war on other nations in order to expand the borders of Israel and to increase its greatness. For a *milhemet mitzvah* [the king] does not need to obtain the permission of the religious court, but goes out to war and compels the nation to go. However, in a *milhemet reshut*, he does not take the nation [to war] without the approval of the religious court [the Sanhedrin]."

How does Maimonides define a *milhemet mitzvah* and a *milhemet reshut*?

How does Maimonides explain a Jewish war of self-defense?

Why does Maimonides make a distinction over who may declare and initiate each of the types of war?

Biblical Sources
To get a sense of Jewish views on war, study Devarim 20:1-18, which is the central biblical statement about war and its limits.

Sotah 44b

"Rava says: everyone agrees that the wars of conquest of Joshua are [examples of] a [*milhemet mitzvah*], whereas the expansionist wars of the Davidic house are *reshut*.

Why do the wars of conquest that Joshua fought fall under the category of *milhemet mitzvah*? How are they different from the wars fought by King David?

Devarim 20:5-9

"And the officers shall speak unto the people, saying: 'What man is there that hath built a new house, and hath not dedicated it? Let him go and return to his house, lest he die in the battle, and another man dedicate it. And what man is there that hath planted a vineyard, and hath not used the fruit thereof? Let him go and return unto his house, lest he die in the battle, and another man use the fruit thereof. And what man is there that hath betrothed a wife, and hath not taken her? Let him go and return unto his house, lest he die in the battle, and another man take her.' And the officers shall speak further unto the people, and they shall say: 'What man is there that is fearful and faint-hearted? Let him go and return unto his house, lest his brethren's heart melt as his heart.' And it shall be, when the officers have made an end of speaking unto the people, that captains of hosts shall be appointed at the head of the people."

What are the four types of people exempt from war?

Do the four exemptions share any common characteristics?

What do you think might be the rationale for these exemptions?

Maimonides, Mishneh Torah, Hilkhot Melakhim 7:4

"In a *milhemet mitzvah* everyone goes out [to war], even a groom from his chambers and a bride from her wedding canopy."

What is Maimonides' interpretation of Devarim?

Why do you think he includes "a bride from her wedding canopy"? (Answer: to emphasize the importance of full participation in a *milhemet mitzvah*.)

Follow-Up and Enrichment

To continue your discussion about Jewish attitudes toward war, explore the ethical questions surrounding battle, and study the text of Devarim 20 as background for a discussion on how soldiers should behave in combat.

Stage a debate about the current crisis in Afghanistan to analyze how the sources inform our understanding of the situation.

Related Resources

www.babaganewz.com — a monthly Jewish magazine and related website for children ages 9-13. See especially the Kislev 5762/November 2001 issue that addresses terrorism both in the magazine and accompanying teacher's guide.

President Bush requested that every American child send $1.00 to help provide aid for the children of Afghanistan. Donations should be sent to:

America's Fund for Afghan Children
c/o The White House
1600 Pennsylvania Avenue
Washington, DC 20509-1600

Dr. David Elcott, author, lecturer, and organizational consultant, has brought his insights and analyses of Judaism and contemporary Jewish life to well over 100 communities across North America. He is the author of A Sacred Journey: The Jewish Quest for a Perfect World.

This lesson plan is reprinted with permission from the Teacher's Guide of BabagaNewz. Copyright 2002, The AVI CHAI Foundation, in partnership with Jewish Family & Life!

Books That Help Us Understand "The Other" and Participate in Repairing Our Broken World

Kathy Bloomfield

Reading with children is one way to open a discussion about Jewish values and understanding people who are different from us.

H ere is a unique collection of books to serve as a resource for people who wish to discuss the trials of our times with children of all ages.

50 Ways to a Safer World : Everyday Actions You Can Take to Prevent Violence in Neighborhoods, Schools, and Communities
By Patricia Occhiuzzo Giggans and Barrie Levy
An all-purpose guide to combating violence and making the world a better place.
Seals Press, 1997/Adult/144pp/PB

Bad Stuff in the News: A Family Guide to Handling the Headlines
By Rabbi Marc Gellman and Monsignor Thomas Hartman

A book to help kids and their parents understand and cope with the scary things kids read and hear about.
Seastar Publishing Company, 2002/Ages 9-12/128pp/HC

Bereaved Children and Teens: A Support Guide for Parents and Professionals
By Earl A. Grollman
Fourteen experts explore the complex problems faced by young mourners.
Beacon Press, 1996/Adult/256pp/PB

Children of Character: A Parent's Guide
By Steven Carr Reuben, Ph.D.
A book to help parents lead their children to ethical choices in everyday life.
Lee Canter & Associates, 1997/Adult/198pp/PB

The Christmas Menorahs: How a Town Fought Hate
By Janice Cohn, Illustrated by Bill Farnsworth
A story of how two children and their families stood together against hate. This true story took place in Billings, Montana, in 1993.
Albert Whitman & Company, 1995/Ages 7-11/40pp/PB

The Cow of No Color: Riddle Stories and Justice Tales from World Traditions
By Nina Jaffe & Steve Zeitlin, Illustrated by Whitney Sherman
Every tale in this outstanding multicultural collection returns to the question What is fair?
Henry Holt & Company, 1998/Age 9+/128pp/HC

Dim Sum, Bagels, and Grits: A Sourcebook for Multicultural Families
By Myra Alperson
An informed, comprehensive guide to raising a multicultural family.
Farrar Straus & Giroux, 2001/Adult/304pp/PB

Golden Rules: The Ten Ethical Values Parents Need to Teach Their Children
By Rabbi Wayne Dosick
Stories, anecdotes, and affirmations that demonstrate universal values.
HarperCollins, 1998 Adult/222pp/PB

In God's Name
By Sandy Eisenberg Sasso, Illustrated by Phoebe Stone
The diversity and unity of people and their search for God.
Jewish Lights Publishing, 1994/Ages 5-10/32pp/HC

Making Loss Matter: Creating Meaning in Difficult Times
By Rabbi David Wolpe
This powerful book explores ways to transform suffering into a source of strength.
Riverhead Books, 2000/Adult/240pp/PB

Rooftop Secrets and Other Stories of Anti-Semitism
By Lawrence Bush, Illustrated by Martin Lemelman
Eight stories featuring children and describing anti-Semitism through the ages.
UAHC Press, 1998/Age 12+/158pp/PB

Shalom, Salaam, Peace
By Howard I. Bogot, Illustrated by Norman Gorbaty
A poetic call for peace in the Middle East and everywhere. Vibrant, bold illustrations are paired with lyrical text in English, Hebrew, and Arabic to transform the book into a global experience.
CCAR Press, 2000/All ages/32pp/PB

The Spirit That Moves Us, Vol. I: A Literature-Based Resource Guide, Teaching About Diversity, Prejudice, Human Rights & the Holocaust
By Rachel Quenk
A resource guide to assist teachers in using children's literature and classroom activities to help children understand the concepts of the Holocaust.
Tilbury House, 1998/Ages 5-10/192pp/PB

The Spirit That Moves Us, Vol. II: A Literature-Based Resource Guide, Teaching About the Holocaust & Human Rights
By Laura R. Petovello
A resource guide for teachers demonstrating how to use children's literature and a wide range of classroom activities to teach the concepts of diversity, culture, community, and human rights.
Tilbury House, 1997/Age 11+/170pp/PB

Tales of Tikkun: New Jewish Stories to Heal the Wounded World
By Phyllis O. Berman & Arthur O. Waskow
A collection of interpretive stories that address important

global issues.
Jason Aronson, 1996/Adult/156pp/PB

Talking About Death: A Dialogue Between Parent and Child

By Earl A. Grollman, Illustrated by Susan Avishai
Sensitive and helpful advice to help parents talk to children about death. Includes a story that can be read together.
Beacon Press, 1991/Adult/118pp/PB

What If the Zebras Lost Their Stripes?

By John Reitano, Illustrated by William Haines
Vibrant pictures and provocative questions in a lively book to discuss differences with the very young.
Paulist Press, 1998/Ages 4-9/32pp/HC

Why?

Written and Illustrated by Nikolai Popov
A wordless picture book about the absurdities of war.
North-South Books, 1996/Ages 4-8/32 pp/PB

Kathy Bloomfield currently works at Jewish Family & Life! Formerly President of For Words Books, a national Jewish book fair company, she is a recognized expert in the field of Jewish children's literature.

High Holiday Reflections

From Deadly Fire to Divine Sparks

Leila Gal Berner

God needs us to manifest godliness and
goodness in the world.

"*Eicha   yashva badad ha-ir rabati am haita k'almana...*"
"Alas! How lonely sits the city once great with people! She that was great among the nations has
become like a widow. . . Bitterly she weeps in the night... All
her inhabitants sigh... From above, God sent a fire down into
my bones... I am left forlorn, in constant misery..."

These are words from the first chapter of the biblical book
Eicha, Lamentations, written about the destruction of
Jerusalem some 2,600 years ago. How powerful they are for
us today. Bitterly, New York weeps in the night; a fire has
rained down into the very marrow of the city's bones. She is
left forlorn.

The devastation of September 11, 2001, that left a gaping
wound in the heart of that great city has devastated all of us.
We have so much to weep about. We feel helpless in the face

76

of the enormity of evil, and sometimes we feel hopeless too. We ache, we weep, and rage burns within us.

On Tuesday, September 11, amidst the whirlwind of my own emotions, I found myself shaking — crying the tears of one who is lost. So many of us experienced that terrible mix of emotions — intense grief and an almost all-consuming anger. So many of us, God help us, have felt the fires of vengeance come alive within us.

What do we do with all the pain and the anger? Many hundreds of years ago, our rabbis inserted a paragraph into the Passover haggadah that begins with the words "Sh'foch chamatcha al ha-goyim asher lo yaduch." "O God, pour out your wrath on the nations who do not know you!" This was our people's cry of rage and our thirst for vengeance, shouted out as we opened the door at our seders to welcome Eliyahu Ha-Navi — Elijah the Prophet, the harbinger of the Messiah, the one who will announce the coming of a time of redemption, peace, and cosmic justice.

What an intriguing combination of words and context. On the one hand, these were the words of a powerless people in the Diaspora, victims of oppression and violence. This was the cry of a people powerless to pour out wrath upon their oppressors. And so we cried out to God, "Punish these monsters, wreak vengeance on our behalf!" And yet, at that very moment we are shouting for revenge, we are welcoming Eliyahu; we look to a time of justice and peace when violence, hatred, and evil would be no more.

There is a message here for us now as we stare into the face of evil — vengeance may be what our hearts ache for at this moment, but justice, repair, and healing must be our ultimate long-term goals.

As our tradition teaches, I believe in punishment for those who perpetrate evil. But there is a profound difference between vengeance and punishment. Vengeance is indiscriminate violence, which may serve to appease our sense of powerlessness but ultimately does not eradicate evil. Vengeance escalates evil, creating new generations of martyrs and survivors who hate even more deeply. Punishment, on the other hand, is a controlled and targeted exercise of just power, directed only against the sources of evil.

Rabbi Richard Hirsch writes, "The Torah suggests that on the night of the 10th plague in Egypt, God let loose an avenging angel, the 'mashchit,' the 'destroyer.' Having let loose this overwhelming power, God now has to be in all Israelite doorways to deflect the 'destroyer.' A 19th-century Eastern European rabbi, Aaron Samuel Tamaret, was puzzled by this aspect of the Exodus story. 'Why,' he asked, 'couldn't God simply program the destroyer to hit the Egyptian homes and avoid those of the Israelites?'"

Rabbi Hirsh's answer: "Once the 'destroyer' is loose, it cannot differentiate between the guilty and the innocent." To Rabbi Hirsch's teaching, I would add: Let that be a lesson to us — careful, deliberate punishment of the perpetrators of evil is necessary, but vengeance against innocents is not. Let our government and our leaders remember that once let loose, the *mashchit* cannot differentiate between the guilty and the innocent.

In these days since the "tremendum," as I have come to think of September 11, in this time since that tremendous, horrible day, I have had moments of deep despair. Like many, I have wondered if despite all I have been taught, human beings are so prone to evil that there is no hope. I have asked myself: Where was God? And why did the "tremendum" crash down upon us? Wrestling with conflicting emotions and questions, I have come to some insights that may help as we all continue to struggle through this dark time.

As for my fellow human beings, I remember that Jewish tradition teaches that every human being is created *b'tzelem Elohim*, in God's image, and that we are fundamentally good. Each morning, we recite the words *Elohai neshama shehnatata bi tehorah hi*. My God, the soul that you have implanted within me is pure. We believe that we come into this world with essential goodness and purity, and we affirm each day that we decide whether we will taint that goodness, whether we will sully our lives.

Jewish tradition also teaches that each of us has within us a *yetzer hatov* and a *yetzer harah*, an inclination toward good and an inclination toward evil. The primary task of our lives is to always ensure that our goodness overwhelms our evil, that our capacity for righteousness defeats our inclination toward sin. In this context, we understand that sin is not only what we do; sin is also what we can become — it can define who we are unless we fight against it.

After the struggles of this week, I do not despair in humankind. I believe that human beings have a greater capacity for good than for evil; it is, however, up to us. While we may become discouraged, feel helpless and hopeless knowing that some humans become evil, we must not despair. Rather, we must take up the challenge posed to us by our ancient rabbis in the Mishnah: "In a place where people descend into depravity, be determined to be decent."

God? Yes, I asked the question — "Where were You?

Where are You?" But it may surprise you to know that my questions quickly transformed into deeply held convictions. Ultimately, I have never believed that God is a power who predetermines all, willing premature death on one and a long and healthy life on another. I have never believed that God is the perpetrator of unjust tragedy.

During his eulogy for his 24-year-old son Alex, who died in a car crash, the famous Protestant minister Reverend William Sloan Coffin said, "Nothing infuriates me more than the incapacity of seemingly intelligent people to get it through their heads that God doesn't go around this world with his finger on triggers, his fist around knives, his hands on steering wheels. God is dead set against all unnatural deaths… My own consolation lies in knowing that it was not the will of God that my son die; that God's heart was the first of all hearts to break."

God was not with the hijackers. God was with the passengers who resisted the terrorists, most probably diverting one plane from crashing into the Capitol or the White House. God was with the hundreds of firefighters and other rescue workers who ran into burning buildings and gave their lives so that others might live. God was with the doctor who pedaled his bicycle from Connecticut to arrive at "ground zero" to save lives and heal wounds. God was with the thousands who gave blood.

Ani ma'aminah b'emunah shleymah, I do believe, with absolute faith, that God is that Power in the universe that energizes us toward the good, toward the best that is within us. I do believe, with absolute faith, that God gives us the courage to stand against evil, to live our lives ethically, to be strong in times of deepest adversity. I do believe, with absolute faith, that God is omnipresent — with us every-where in our world, and omni-beneficent — the greatest power for good in our world. Even so, though it may seem like heresy to say so, I am not sure that God is omnipotent, all powerful. Like Rabbi Abraham Joshua Heschel, I believe that God needs us to manifest godliness and goodness in the world. I believe that God calls out to us, cries out to us, beseeches us to respond to the Divine challenge. For without us, God is divinity *in potentio* — the Holy only becomes man-ifest through us and our actions. That is what God's gift of free will is all about. In Rabbi Heschel's words, "We are not asked to abandon life and to say farewell to this world, but to keep the spark within aflame, and to allow God's light to be reflected in our own faces. God is waiting on every road that leads from intention to action."

If this is indeed so, then how can we relate to the awesome words of Rosh Hashanah from the prayer *"U'netaneh tokef,"* "On Rosh Hashanah it is written, and on Yom Kippur it is sealed ... Who shall live and who shall die"? Is this really a prayer about predestination, about God's final (and seem-ingly arbitrary) decision to spare some of us and afflict oth-ers? If it were, how could we sing it each year with sincerity, without shaking our fist at heaven and saying, "This is unfair, unjust!" How could we not protest that such a God is unwor-thy of our faith, our trust, our love?

I believe that *"U'netaneh tokef"* offers us a very different message. To me, it speaks about uncertainty, about the fragility of life, about the arbitrary whims of nature that God created but cannot entirely control. Sometimes people die young, ravaged by disease. Sometimes nature is savage and destructive, and even God cannot stop the savagery.

But what of the catastrophes we cause by our savagery? What power do we have over life and death? Does God write us into the Book of Life or Death? Or are we the authors of our own destinies? A thousand years ago, Rabbi Bahya ibn Paquda wrote: "Days are like scrolls. Write on them what you want remembered." God has given us the precious gift of free will, and God has given us our outrage at injustice, our feelings of compassion for those who are suffering. To paraphrase Rabbi Harold Kushner, author of *When Bad Things Happen to Good People*, responding to life's unfairness is a reflection of God's compassion and anger working through us. This may be the surest proof of God's reality and power.

Despite its language of royalty and judgment, the prayer *U'netaneh tokef* teaches us a powerful lesson about life's uncertainty. Its concluding words are crucial: "*teshuvah, tefilla, tzedakah*" — inward turning, prayer or yearning, and acts of righteous and just caring — avert the severity of the decree. In the end, action is what matters — how we live. Rabbi Heschel's words again echo with profound truth: God asks us to keep the [Divine] spark within us aflame, to fill our lives with acts of righteousness and goodness. "God is waiting on every road that leads from intention to action."

A few days ago, I wept again, this time in gratitude and awe. A young man whom I have never met gave this gift to me. His story exemplifies what life is all about, what our task as human beings is all about, what reflecting God in our actions really means.

"My name is Usman Farman," the young man wrote. "I graduated from Bentley with a Finance degree last May. I am 21 years old, turning 22 in October. I am Pakistani and I am Muslim. Until September 11, 2001, I worked at the World

Trade Center... I have friends and acquaintances [who also work there]. Some remain buried under the rubble." Usman described in great detail what he saw and heard that day, but there is one piece of his story that I most want to share with you. "We were evacuated to the north side of building #7, still only a block from the towers. [We were told] to go north and not to look back. Five city blocks later, I stopped and turned around to watch. With a thousand people staring, we saw in shock as the first tower collapsed... The next thing I remember is that a dark cloud of glass and debris about 50 stories high came tumbling toward us... I turned around and ran as fast as possible and I fell down trying to get away... I was on my back, facing this massive cloud... Everything was already dark... I normally wear a pendant around my neck inscribed with an Arabic prayer for safety. [While I was on the ground, with people stampeding past me], a Hassidic Jewish man came up to me and held the pendant in his hand and looked at it. He read the Arabic out loud for a second. What he said next, I will never forget. With a deep Brooklyn accent, he said, "Brother, if you don't mind, there is a cloud of glass coming at us, grab my hand, and let's get the hell out of here." He helped me stand up and we ran for what seemed like forever without looking back. He was the last person I would ever have thought would help me. If it weren't for him, I probably would have been engulfed in shattered glass and debris."

In one instant of profound humanity, in one flash of profound goodness, the cloud of glass that pursued Usman and so many others became transformed from a rain of evil into a shower of righteousness — the shards of glass, deadly splinters caused by indescribable evil were redeemed and they became shards of light, sparks of the Divine, manifest in one human being.

Remember that you can bring about *tikkun olam*, the healing and redemption of our shattered world. Remember that you do manifest God and good. For in each and every moment of our lives, we can bring healing, we can save a world. This is our hope, this is our challenge, this is how we can enter the New Year choosing life over death, affirming good even in the face of the darkest of all evils.

"On Rosh Hashanah it is written and on Yom Kippur it is sealed." How shall we live as this New Year unfolds? *Chizku v'imtzu*: be strong and of good courage — and may each of us be inscribed in the Book of a Good Life in the coming days.

Rabbi Leila Gal Berner was ordained at the Reconstructionist Rabbinical College and holds a doctorate in medieval Jewish history from the University of California at Los Angeles. She serves as Co-rabbi of Congregation Bet Mishpachah in Washington, D.C., an egalitarian synagogue embracing a diversity of sexual and gender identities. Rabbi Berner also teaches in the Women's Studies and Jewish Studies programs at George Washington University.

Transcending the Evil Decree

Ronne Friedman

*Upon the ashes of the Temple, the rabbis
constructed a new faith and a new culture.*

No single piece of poetic liturgy for the High Holy Days has haunted me more during my career than the *U'netaneh Tokef,* which is recited on both Rosh Hashanah and Yom Kippur. Although probably composed in the Byzantine period, subsequent Jewish legend attributed it to a certain Rabbi Amnon of Mayence, heralded as a martyr of the First Crusade. Rabbi Amnon was purported to have spoken these words as he was put to the stake.

The theme, you will recall, is the awesome power of this day during which God as Divine Judge determines the destiny of every human being.

"As the shepherd seeks out the flock,
and makes the sheep pass under the staff,
so do You muster and number and consider every soul,
setting the bounds of every creature's life,

and decreeing its destiny.
On Rosh Hashanah it is written,
On Yom Kippur it is sealed:
How many shall pass on, how many shall come to be;
Who shall live and who shall die;
Who shall see ripe age and who shall not;
Who shall perish by fire and who by water;
Who by sword and who by beast;
Who by hunger and who by thirst;
Who by earthquake and who by plague;
Who by strangling and who by stoning;
Who shall be secure and who shall be driven;
Who shall be tranquil and who shall be troubled;
Who shall be poor and who shall be rich;
Who shall be humbled and who exalted.
But *t'shuvah*, repentance, *t'fillah*, prayer, and *tzedakah*, righteous giving, temper judgment's severe decree."

These words have exacted an uneasy hold on me throughout my rabbinate. I have always emphatically rejected the theological implications of a literal interpretation of this prayer. Simply stated, I do not subscribe to a belief that personifies God not only as cosmic judge, but also as willing executioner or even worse, as willful torturer. Nevertheless, read as a metaphor for the fragility of our lives, I am overwhelmed by the exquisite and magnificent power of these words. They have never seemed more true to me than during the past two weeks.

Consider this transposition:

Who took a day off, and who appeared for work;

Who was held up in a traffic jam, and who arrived on time;

Ronne Friedman

Who boarded a flight, having missed a plane the day before, and who cancelled a trip because of a family emergency;

Who worked on the 26th floor and who on the 104th;

Who was late because of a teacher's meeting and who happened to have an appointment with a broker at the World Trade Center that day;

Who by fire and who by falling debris;

Who by smoke and who by jumping;

Who escaped, and who was led to safety;

Who died a hero in the line of duty, and who spent days and nights searching for him;

Which families are bereaved and which relieved.

But what are we to make of the traditional climax to this litany, "*u'tshuvah*, But repentance, *u'tefillah*, prayer, *u'tzedakah*, and righteous giving, *ma'avirin*, temper, *et roa hagezerah*, judgment's severe decree?" Do we show up to pray, commit ourselves to moral self-improvement, or give *tzedakah* simply because we imagine that by so doing, our lives will be spared? I don't believe so, and neither do you. In moments of stress and trauma, we may be tempted to revert to adolescent fantasies, to envisioning God in the guise of a celestial Monty Hall with whom we can make a deal, but our rational selves know better.

Permit me to suggest an alternative reading that will provide a more comfortable theological path. I would amend the text to read: "With *tshuvah*, with prayer, and with *tzedakah*, we transcend the severe decree." How is that so? What is the significance of the tripartite formulation of *tshuvah*, prayer, and *tzedakah*? What do those activities have in common? Only this — as we engage in *tshuvah*, prayer, and *tzedakah,* we are committed to a vision that reaches beyond the narrow confines of self. Each behavior is predicated upon a belief in something greater than ourselves. *Tshuvah,* prayer, and *tzedakah* are future oriented, rooted in hope for the future, in faith that there will be a future and expressed as personal responsibility to ensure that future. Acts of *tshuvah,* prayer, and *tzedakah* will grant us neither impunity nor immunity, but it is through these behaviors that we transcend the divine decree, our fragility, our finitude, our fate.

Jews are schooled to respond to catastrophe. In the first Christian century, our people confronted a national calamity of epic proportions. The revolt against Rome was an abject failure. The army was destroyed, Jerusalem turned into a pile of rubble, families and friends were dislocated.

The Temple, national symbol of religion, culture, and commerce, was obliterated. As Rabbi Yohanan ben Zakkai and his disciple, Rabbi Joshua, fled the burning city, the disciple looked upon the destroyed Temple and cried out, "Woe to us! The place where Israel [sacrificed and thereby] received atonement for sins is in ruins!" Rabbi Yochanan replied: "My son, do not be distressed. We have an atonement just as effective, that is, the practice of loving deeds." Though they had suffered the most grievous loss imaginable, the rabbis of the Talmud offered concrete means by which the individual and the people could rise above the immediate disaster. In addition to loving deeds, *tzedakah,* prayer, and *tshuvah,* were added to the list of substitutes for sacrifice that could now affect atonement. In other words, the rabbis refused to accept the most terrible catastrophe that they could imagine as proof of the apocalypse. They insisted that this was not the end of days, the concluding chapter in temporal history. The rabbis knew that the people could stand against the apocalypse only by committing themselves to a program of restorative action. If that action could not be realized on a political plane, then it would have to find its expression in the interior space of heightened spirituality and moral sensibility. Upon the ashes of the Temple, they constructed a new faith and culture, and created the structure of Judaism that in its essence survives to this day.

Psychoanalyst Viktor Frankl, a survivor of the Holocaust, echoed similar sentiments when he wrote, "...Survival cannot be the supreme value. Unless life points to something beyond itself, survival is pointless and meaningless. It is not even possible. This is the very lesson that I learned in three years spent in Auschwitz and Dachau, ... Only those who were oriented toward the future, toward a goal in the future, toward a meaning to fulfill in the future, were likely to survive ... And I think that this is not only true for the survival of individuals, but also holds true for the survival of mankind."

Our media are replete with tales of the heroism of September 11. I have found these three images particularly compelling, for each one is a tale of transcendence built upon a unique vision of the future. The first image is that of five men on United Airlines Flight 93, Jeremy Glick, Thomas Burnett, Jr., Mark Bingham, Todd Beamer, and Lou Nacke. In cell phone contact with family members and a telephone operator, they learned what had happened to the World Trade Towers. Determined not to permit a similar event, they, and possibly others, apparently stormed the hijackers, thereby preventing the probable destruction of another terrorist target. Despite the frenzied tumult of their last moments, they communicated their love for their families. "Tell her I love her and the boys," Todd Beamer told Lisa Jefferson, the telephone operator whom he reached. Jeremy Glick told his wife, Lyz, that he hoped that she would have a good life and take care of their three-month-old baby daughter. Todd Beamer asked Lisa Jefferson to recite the Lord's Prayer with him, and then the team sprang into action, each with a vision of his posterity inspiring his decision.

The second image is that of New York City firefighters and police who responded to the call and entered the World Trade Towers amidst the swirling chaos. What made them risk their lives to save others? From what source did they draw their extraordinary courage? Were they not impelled by a commitment to duty and a sense of honor? They shared a faith in an ordered society based on the rule of law, as well as a belief in the value of service to others by which they overcame their fear and concern for their own personal safety.

G. K. Chesterton once wrote, "The true soldier fights not because he hates what is in front of him, but because he loves what is behind him." Firefighters, police, and daring passengers on a doomed flight shared values predicated upon trust in the future and belief in the meaningfulness of life.

The third image is that of an Orthodox Jew who worked on one of the upper floors of the North Tower. Realizing that he was trapped and would not escape, he phoned his wife, expressed his love, and then called kosher witnesses to tell them that his chance of survival was nonexistent. He did so in order that his wife should escape a terrible fate created by a painful problem in Jewish law. A woman whose husband is presumed dead, but without proof of the fact, is not permitted to remarry. She is called an *agunah*, someone who is forbidden to other men because her marriage has not been formally dissolved by death or divorce. For this devout Jewish man, the prospect of consigning his wife to such a status, given the likelihood that his body would never be recovered, prompted him to use his last minutes on earth to protect her. By arranging witnesses, he could be assured that she would have the prerogative to remarry. Despite the knowledge that his life would end, he turned his spirit toward the future and refused to permit his widow to be added to his funeral pyre. His last message, too, was a clarion call to choose life.

More than two weeks have passed since the catastrophe of September 11. We have moved through the first stages of shock and disbelief. We no longer wake up in the morning hoping that what occurred was, in fact, a nightmare that will evanesce as the sun rises. We have accepted the painful reality, but we are still uncertain about what to do next. How can we put the pieces of the world that we knew back together?

Permit me a story that concerns a mother and her daughter. The daughter was unoccupied and sought her mother's attention. The mother, however, a busy professional, was desperate to finish some of her work. To occupy the girl's time, she gave her a pencil and paper and said, "Here, sweetheart, go and draw our family." Two minutes later the daughter returned with a picture — all stick figures. The mother, trying to buy some more time, gave her another piece of paper and said, "Now go and draw the dog." In two minutes the child was back with another stick figure. The mother felt guilty and exasperated. Torn between her obligations to work and the imploring eyes of her daughter, she picked up a magazine. On the back cover, she saw a map of the world. In what she thought was a stroke of genius, the mother ripped out the picture of the world and tore it into small jig-saw puzzle pieces. She turned to her daughter and said, "Here, my love, is a puzzle I made for you, go and put the world back together." Of course, you know what happened. Not five minutes later, the little girl was back displaying her work with a sense of great accomplishment: "Mommy, Mommy, look what I have done." And the mother looked and with an admixture of chagrin and pride asked, "Darling, how did you put the world together so quickly?" The daughter answered, "Mommy, it was easy. There was a picture of a man on the back and once I put him all together the world fell into place." If we would wish our broken world to fall into place, we must begin the task by reassembling ourselves — that is the message of Yom Kippur.*

Elie Wiesel has written: "When God created us, God gave Adam a secret — and that secret was not how to begin, but how to begin again. In other words, it is not given to us to begin; that privilege is God's alone. But it is given to us to begin again — and we do every time we choose to defy death and side with the living."

U'tshuvah, by turning toward recovery, u'tfillah, with prayers that our recovery inspire a renewal of shattered spirits and a reunification of our broken world, u'tzedakah, may we rekindle the light of righteous actions and loving deeds. M'kor Hachayim, Source of all life, Harachaman, Source of all mercy, grant us the grace to transcend the evil that our eyes have witnessed, to begin again, and to replace it with good.
Keyn y'hi ratzon.

*I owe a debt of gratitude to my dear friend Rabbi Douglas Krantz of Armonk, New York, from whom I heard the story of the mother and daughter. I don't know its origin. I had heard a similar parable concerning a father and son several years ago, but I was unable to discover the original source.

———————

Ronne Friedman is Senior Rabbi of Temple Israel in Brookline, Massachusetts. He has also served as rabbi to Temple Beth Zion in Buffalo, New York.

Moments of Eternity

David Glanzberg-Krainin

*Heroism is about sacrificing something
essential for something beyond oneself.*

On the afternoon of September 11, 2001, and since then, we have caught a glimpse of eternity. Since those horrible events, we seem to better understand that some aspects of life are trivial and fleeting, while others are of utmost importance and contain within them an aspect of eternity. I by no means wish to claim that this is the silver lining in that horrible cloud that was unleashed by the atrocities that our nation experienced. But I have the sense that many of you, like me, have been aware of a shift in the priorities of this nation since the horrendous events of the morning of September 11. And in that shift, I think we have uncovered a reality that much of what had previously consumed us as a nation contains an element of triviality at its core.

It is said that crisis can bring out the best in an individual

94

and in a nation. We have witnessed some stunning examples of heroism and bravery — acts of kindness both large and small.

My question to each one of us is: How do we make consciousness of the eternal (i.e., the awareness of what is truly important in life) not just a reaction to horror, but a day-to-day series of choices that apply to how we live in times of crisis as well as in times of peace and calm? For in many ways, I believe that this question is at core the question of Yom Kippur, the day on which we try to strip life down to its essence and see ourselves and our lives for what they really are.

In some very positive ways, America is a very different country than it was a few months ago. In no way am I minimizing the wounds we have suffered. Yes, we are more afraid to fly. Yes, our economy has suffered a blow. Yes, our sense of safety has been threatened. But this country has changed in the aftermath of the atrocities, and in many ways, we have become a better people as a result.

Let me give you some examples of what I mean. A month ago, America had a pretty shallow understanding of who our heroes were. We were quick to equate heroism and celebrity. We were debating whether or not it was fair that our sports stars were seen as role models by our children. Parents of girls were lamenting the fact that back-to-school clothes were tighter and more revealing than ever because of the influence of Britney Spears and teenie-bopper music icons. We were absorbed in the latest scandal of the moment: Who, we wondered, would Connie Chung be interviewing next?

But since September 11 our heroes have changed. Now, we remember that the men and women of this country who put on uniforms each day — our police officers and our fire-fighters — are the men and women who responded to the carnage. Now we remember that firefighters are not just people who threaten to walk off the job because their medical benefits are being cut.

We used to think that our heroes were the fund managers of securities firms. After September 11, we recognized that the true hero of one brokerage firm was not the fund manager, but the security chief. The former Vietnam vet who made sure that every worker in his firm's offices had managed to get out of the building. Only when he had made sure that everyone else had gotten out, did he try to leave — only by then it was too late.

There were ordinary travelers who, on the morning of September 11, had to make an extraordinary decision: whether to hope against hope for some escape from the horror of the hijacking or to attack the hijackers and bring down the plane. People who, after learning from cell phone conversations with their loved ones that the purpose of the hijacking was to make the plane into a huge bomb, rushed the hijackers and brought down the plane in a field in south-west Pennsylvania, aware that everyone aboard would die but saving the lives of hundreds, if not thousands, of others in the process.

On September 11 we learned an important truth about the nature of heroism. It's about sacrificing something essential for something beyond just oneself. It has very little to do with fame and fortune.

Celebrity and fame can come and go. On September 11, we discovered that so often it's the unseen and the unrecognized who are our society's true heroes.

Sometimes it may be hard to remember that in God's eyes, both the CEO of the brokerage firm and the receptionist are made in the image of the Divine, and that both lives have infinite value.

Each is a parent of a child who longs to hear a voice on the other end of the phone saying that you are okay. And both, should you have the misfortune of not making it out of the building alive, will leave behind broken hearts of the people with whom you have shared your lives. And there will be an aching void for those who loved you.

On that stairwell in the World Trade Center, seeing the fear and pain on the face of your receptionist and co-worker, recognizing in that face your own pain and fear, the meaning and the preciousness of both of your lives became evident. That was a moment of eternity. That's when you saw the world from God's perspective.

Eternity was found when we climbed out of the walls of our own self-absorption and realized that we belonged to something larger than just ourselves and our immediate families. In the aftermath of terror, we realize that the only thing that matters is that our children are alive and okay. Instead of racing through a take-out dinner between soccer and an SAT preparation class, we came home for dinner. And then the whole family went to the synagogue to gain strength from the presence of a community and from the power of prayer. And after the service, you called the Red Cross and made appointments for everyone to donate blood.

By the next night, around the dinner table, each member of the family talked about giving up something he or she enjoyed temporarily — taking the money that was usually spent on recreation or fun and instead donating that money as *tzedakah* to one of the organizations helping the victims of the disaster. As family members sat around the table figuring out what they were going to do without for just a short while, there was a moment of eternity. A moment when your family came face to face with the fact that their lives are a great gift, and in response to that recognition, they realized that they could give something to those who were hurting. In that moment of awareness, they saw the world from God's perspective. That was a moment of eternity.

And I have the sense that all across this nation, many of us, perhaps for the first time in a long time, sensed a moment of eternity. Perhaps it was during the time that we were driving to work. And perhaps instead of being a Type-A personality with Type-A driving habits, we found ourselves driving in the right lane of the expressway, slowing down and signaling to those cars trying to merge onto the highway that they were free to go ahead of us. It was not a big deal. You might get to the office four minutes later than usual, but then there would be a lot less sweat on your palms when you arrived.

As you waited for coffee at Au Bon Pain, the slow pace of the man behind the counter did not get on your nerves as it usually did. Maybe he was moving slowly because this was his second job of the day, when you felt refreshed after your morning workout at the gym. And in the span of time that you were wondering about that, and taking the time to thank him sincerely for the coffee, and then finding you had dropped an extra dollar in his tip jar, you may just have had a moment of eternity. Because it was then that you realized that all those people whom you let in to the expressway ahead of you were just people like you trying to get to work.

And this guy who had dragged his feet to get your morning coffee was like you as well — someone trying to support himself and his family. And at that moment, you realized that you had a lot in common. And when you came to that awareness, you experienced the world from God's perspective. That was your moment of eternity.

In the aftermath of those moments of horror, we have been graced with a different kind of perspective. It's as though the knocking down of the Twin Towers left us with access to Windows on the World. In the last two weeks, we've managed to view the world high above the places we normally inhabit. And the world that we see from that view has changed the way we live.

But now, here's the question: How long will it last? How long will we see the world from the perspective of eternity? What will sustain us after those wonderful moments of grace have passed, and we are back to rushing to get our teenager from soccer practice, and driving a little too closely to the car in front of us during the morning rush? How do we turn these moments of eternity into the fabric of our lives, rather than make them momentary pauses?

Of course, I would like to give you an answer. I would like to tell you that I have a simple formula. Wouldn't it be great if there were a simple formula? We could all go down to the book store — or log on to Amazon.com — and order a book with a title like *Hanging On to Those Moments of Eternity: 10 Ways to Turn Catastrophe into Spiritual Fulfillment*. If only life could be reduced to a self-help book. As we all know, there is no simple formula.

There's an author I like very much. Her name is Anne Lamott. One of her books is a meditation on life called *Bird by Bird.* In the book, Lamott remembers a scene from her childhood in which her 10-year-old brother had been given an assignment to write an in-depth report about birds. It was a major assignment, one he had been given months to work on, but he was paralyzed by the prospects of even starting. When her brother, almost at the point of despair, cried to her father, "I can't do this. It's too big of an assignment," the father responded, "Just do it one step at a time, bird by bird."

That's good advice: Bird by bird. It will resonate with any-one who has experienced recovery as "one day at a time."

This is what Judaism answers as well. It's not in the moments of catastrophe; it's not even, necessarily, in the fleeting moments of grace in which God's presence is felt as surely as a partner's touch. The Jewish way is the way of the everyday. Living a Jewish life means bringing a level of holi-ness to this world, to this life, to this very day.

That's really the task we've come to remind ourselves about on this evening at the start of Yom Kippur. Yom Kippur gives us tools to begin the process. We know that fasting is a helpful tool; we know that time in reflection and contemplation is a helpful tool; we know that time to con-front our own lives with honesty and humility is a helpful tool. But unless we turn these 25 hours into something more, into something sustaining in our lives, they are no more sig-nificant than a momentary bout of compassion during the afternoon rush hour.

The purpose of this Yom Kippur is to point us in the direc-tion of eternity. We take ourselves out of our lives, out of our infatuation with the material, out of our obsession with food; out of our desires for sex. We meditate for one day each year about what really matters. And we do this not as a

Sisyphean exercise in absurdity — not so we have one day on the calendar to imagine a different life with different values and different priorities. No, we go through this exercise of Yom Kippur to gain a measure of eternity, and then to gird ourselves for living in an unredeemed world in which the measure of eternity seems very far away.

Of course, Jewish tradition doesn't expect us to go through the year with one giant dose of eternity on Yom Kippur and the hope that it will sustain us until next Yom Kippur. Instead, Jewish tradition offers us a multitude of paths to eternity along the way, each and every day: Shabbat dinner with family and friends when the stresses of the week are left behind; a system of *b'rakhot*, or blessings that note and give thanks for everything from the bread we eat to the gift of waking from sleep; a system of laws about permissible food that demands that we be conscious before we eat; an obligation to give of our resources through *tzedakah* so that we concretize our awareness that sharing with others is part of a system of justice.

Being a Jew means glimpsing eternity from the food on my plate to the pain on the face of my neighbor. Being a Jew means glimpsing eternity from the understanding of a verse in the Torah and from teaching a new immigrant how to read English.

Yom Kippur tells us that eternity is a lot closer than we think. It's how we live in the day-to-day; it's the everyday acts of *kedusha* — holiness — that make all the difference.

Jewish tradition tells us that there's a tremendous amount of triviality in our day-to-day lives. We don't need a national disaster to remind us of what really matters: the family and friends and community that form the fabric of our lives; the prayer book in our hands that reminds us that God is waiting; reminding us that the words of Torah contained in the *Chumash* that serve as our guideposts for how to live and how to make moral choices.

We don't need a disaster to teach us how to glimpse eternity. Eternity is sitting right here in front of us, if only we would open our eyes, and begin to act — bird by bird.

Rabbi David Glanzbeg-Krainin is a native of Long Island, New York, and received his B.A. from Brown University magna cum laude. A graduate of the Jewish Theological Seminary of America, he has served as Co-chair of the West Chester Area Religious Council, and as Vice President of the Philadelphia Boards of Rabbis. He currently serves as Trustee of the Lasko Family Foundation. He and his wife, Rabbi Deborah Glanzberg-Krainin, are the parents of three children.

A Bible's View of Living in a New and Fearful World

Edwin C. Goldberg

What is the religious response at a time of tragedy?

On the day after September 11, Alex Chadwick, a correspondent for National Public Radio, put it succinctly: "We Americans," he said, "woke up today in a new country." We woke up in a country where the unthinkable could happen, where the very essence of our American way of life could be threatened. And we knew that things would never be the same. Our innocence, our belief that America was different, somehow protected by two oceans, has been lost forever. We are a new and chastened people living in a new and fearful world.

For Jews, however, especially if we have visited Israel, this world seems hauntingly familiar. We know all too well that feeling of emotional quicksand, when every day is filled with uncertainty and dread, and where, in an instant, our lives can change forever. Writing on September 12 in the *New York*

Times, Clyde Haberman spoke the words on many Israeli lips when he asked, "Do you [Americans] get it now?" This question isn't meant to be a smart-alecky response to our tragedy. It's not meant to be a "We told you so." It simply reflects a country that has had to live with terrorists for so long. Unfortunately, as of September 11, America and Israel are members of the same bitter fraternity. It's no longer a matter of reading in the papers of someone else's nightmare. Now it's personal. And we grieve for all who lost their lives in this horrific and cowardly act. To their families we offer our prayers and compassion.

What is the religious response at such times of tragedy? There are actually many responses: prayer, silence, coming together as a community, turning to our sacred texts. When the disaster struck, and I had a moment to reflect on its implications, I turned to our religious writings to find perspective. The first text I read, from the prophet Jeremiah, was filled with pain for those suffering from dreams destroyed. The prophet, who witnessed the catastrophic destruction of Jerusalem 2,500 years ago, declared, "My joy is gone, grief is upon me, my heart is sick. Hark, the cry of my poor people from far and wide in the land: 'Is the Lord not among us? The harvest is past, the summer is ended, we have not been saved.' Because my people is shattered I am shattered; I am dejected, seized by desolation ... Thus said the Lord of Hosts: Listen! Summon the dirge-singers, let them come. Send for the weeping women, let them come. Let them quickly start a wailing for us, that our eyes may run with tears, our pupils flow with water."

The pain and sorrow that Jeremiah felt seems so real to all of us now, witnessing this era's own unspeakable catastrophes. But we feel more than pain. We also feel contempt for the enemies of our people. And so we also identify with these words from the Bible: "He who sows the wind will reap the whirlwind." Those who engage in vile acts of wanton terror and murder will be brought to justice. For we will not rest until such justice is served.

As I considered the magnitude of this past week, I also thought about other role models in the Bible and how they responded to tragedy. David's lament for Jonathan and Saul, "O how the mighty have fallen," made me think of the firefighters and police officers who gave their lives in New York, or the brave passengers who managed to divert the fourth plane from its murderous course. I also remembered the countless people who have come forward to help sift through the rubble, give blood, or counsel the grieving families. All of them are heroes.

I came across a *midrash,* or rabbinical comment, from 2,000 years ago. According to this *midrash,* three biblical characters lived through unthinkable disasters. Each of them witnessed great catastrophes.

Noah saw the destruction of the world through a flood. Daniel saw the destruction of the Temple in Jerusalem. And Job saw the destruction of his family and his home. Unfortunately, all three characters lived through experiences that, thousands of years later, still resonate, especially now.

These days, it's far too easy to identify with Noah. Like him, we have witnessed the destruction of the world as we knew it. True, most buildings in America are still standing. And the flood waters have not swallowed us up. But certainly our lives will never be the same. According to the Bible, Noah's world was destroyed because of *hamas,* which translates as "evil" in the verse. Unfortunately, we associate the word *hamas* with the root evil of our present circumstances. Maybe Islamic terror groups like Hamas weren't directly responsible for what happened here, but their dancing in the streets as our people were dying sends us a clear message: these people are our common enemy. Their hatred cannot be tolerated.

In one way, Noah was luckier than we, for he was able to see the rainbow. He received the promise that never again would the world be destroyed by flood. We are still waiting for that rainbow. We have yet to greet a new and better world. The hatred and envy, unimagined cruelty, still reign and will reign for the foreseeable future. I grieve therefore for ourselves and our children.

If we can identify with Noah, we can also relate to Daniel. For in our age the destruction of religion is rampant. Yes, people worship, and many believe in a good and loving God. This past week we have seen religion console and inspire many of us. But religion is also abused in horrific ways. People blaspheme God by praying words they never practice. Their weekday lives don't reflect the piety of Friday, Saturday, or Sunday. And the worst by far are those with the chutzpah to claim that their acts of terror are in the name of God. Shame on any religious leader who sends terrorists out in the name of God. Such acts threaten the integrity of all religion.

Likewise, those who try to explain that God has a plan for us that includes such suffering miss the point. God doesn't want such suffering. But God has created a world with free choice and, unfortunately, there will be monsters who use their freedom to undermine what genuine religion holds dear. The Jerry Falwells and Pat Robertsons, who have the audacity to claim that the terrorists were aided by a vindictive God, angry at America, should be ashamed. Not only do they blame the victims, they attack the integrity of religion and turn God into a hideous creature.

God is neither sitting above and judging us, meting out punishment for our sins, nor sending the terrorists into action. God is in the compassion we feel for all the bereaved children, parents, spouses, siblings, and friends. God is in the sympathy and support that friends give to the survivors. God is in our resolve to apprehend those responsible for these heinous deeds. God is in the healing that will come slowly but surely to those in grief. And God is in the power of the human spirit to rise above sadness and rededicate our lives to remembering and rebuilding.

Noah was able to see a rainbow and have hope. Daniel, according to tradition, was able to see the Temple destroyed but also rebuilt. Will we see a world in which false practitioners of religion are discredited as charlatans? Will we see religion understood throughout the world as a cradle of compassion and peace? Will we see a world where God is understood as one who suffers with us, and not the cause of our suffering?

If we can identify with Noah and with Daniel, then we can also identify with Job. Like Job, we have seen people's lives destroyed. Like Job we are left with questions rather than answers. But, unlike Job, whom God did visit, we feel alone and abandoned during our time of grief.

Job's questions still resonate in our ears: Why do bad things happen to good people? Why did God create a world of so much pain and misery? How do we explain the injustice and cruelty we see, especially now?

Noah, Daniel, and Job, like us, have seen the world flooded with hate. We have seen religion abused and sullied, families destroyed. The Hebrew word that comes to mind is *churban* — the destruction of everything we thought we knew.

In a sermon delivered almost eighty years ago, Rabbi Israel Levinthal spoke of these three role models. At the time, the world was recovering from the First World War. The lessons of these models are still relevant. Each saw destruction and rebuilding, death and rebirth. We have seen destruction and death, and await the rebuilding and rebirth. We cannot wait for God to start this process; we must take it on ourselves. We must work to build bridges of tolerance and understanding. We must reach out for others. We must better protect our children and our businesses, our synagogues and homes. And we must understand that we can only be effective by working together.

Like Noah, our universe will never be the same. But we can establish safer airports and cities. And we can work with like-minded nations to eradicate the worst offenders of terrorism.

Like Daniel, we have seen religion blasphemed. But we can dedicate ourselves to blending responsibly the realities of our time and the religious insights of our tradition.

And like Job, we have seen terrible calamities befall us. But we can dedicate ourselves to comforting those in sorrow while we strengthen the bonds of our own family. We can learn to never take each other for granted, and to struggle on, even with our broken faith and doubts, somehow knowing that God is good, that God cares, and that even in our pain

Edwin C. Goldberg

God is with us.

After the Revolutionary War, a young Jewish father said to his son, "We have the world to begin again." Rosh Hashanah is the birthday of the world. Every Rosh Hashanah is a time of new beginning. Alex Chadwick was right. We have awakened — to a new and fearful world. We pray that God will help us live with hope to resume our lives, to rebuild our buildings, and to restore our faith in the power of humanity. We hope that this great nation will rise above fear and greet the world again as a place of dreams and blessings.

Edwin C. Goldberg is Rabbi of Temple Judea in Coral Gables, Florida. He is author of the book Midrash for Beginners *and the upcoming* Heads and Tales: Stories of the Sages to Enlighten Our Minds. *He is also the current President of the Rabbinical Association of Greater Miami.*

The Yom Kippur World Order: Inner Piety Through Foul-Smelling Neighbors

Asher Lopatin

The incense comes from the entire public, not just from the Righteous Jew. And every spice must be in it.

Biyshiva shel ma'ala, u'vyshiva shel matah, al da'at hamakom ve'al da'at hakahal, anu matirim l'hitpalel im ha'avaryanim:

In the heavenly, angelic court, and in the earthly, human court; with the consent of God and the consent of our community; we remove all barriers to davening with sinners.

We've all come here, and to countless synagogues throughout the world, to daven together, to cry together, to reach God together. Even if Shabbat is the holiest day of the year, Yom Kippur is the most spiritually intense day of the year. On Shabbat we eat, sleep, shmooze, host guests at our tables, and go on walks. But today, for the next 25 hours, we rise to the heavens as angels — and we bring the heavens down here.

We know only too well what the background is for this

heavenly journey this year — terror, fear, sadness, bewilderment. Our country is searching for a way to protect us from crop dusters and hijacked planes and infiltrators and things too scary to contemplate. It is just too painful to think of how deeply people hate us — we Jews, Americans, lovers of Israel, lovers of freedom. Can we learn anything from the evil directed against us? Surprisingly, I think we can, especially if we take a quick look at who are those who can't stand us.

I spent many years studying Islam and Islamic fundamentalism. It was a long time ago, and there were many aspects which I did not explore. Even though I had thought many times about going into the field of Middle East policy, using my small expertise in Islam, my heart and soul demanded that I pursue being a rabbi, serving the Jewish community. Nor have I ever regretted this decision — even today, when understanding the mind of Islamic terrorists could be helpful for our world. I give this sketch of my life only to introduce the small bit of Islam which I wish to share with you this evening. It is presented in small part to shed some light on the current world situation, but much more importantly to teach us how to act as Jews, as a community which has come together to share and observe together on Yom Kippur.

There are many things that typify Islamic fundamentalism, but what leads to its intolerance? What leads any fundamentalist, for that matter, not to tolerate someone who differs? I want to argue tonight that it is not piety that makes them intolerant. Fundamentalists may be sincere believers. In fact, in my studies of Islamic fundamentalism, it was always clear that the leaders were not just opportunists, but really believed what they preached, what they interpreted in the Qur'an.

They believed that Islam demanded that they copy the prophet Muhammad in protecting the domain of Islam, and in creating the proper environment for maintaining pristine Islamic worship. Many of these fundamentalists are what we would call religiously committed and observant people. Murder for them is a legitimate weapon — and that goes against everything our pious tradition calls for — but it is not piety alone that leads them to justify murdering innocent, unknown people half a world away. In fact, throughout the Middle Ages, and up until the 20th century, there was a deeply pious tradition of Sufism — literally, "the wearers of wool" — which embodied tolerance, acceptance of other paths to God, and oneness with religious people from other religions.

Vestiges of this remain in the Islamic tradition, as seen in the common Muslim practice of visiting the graves of *tzadikim* — righteous Jews and Christians — because these people are accepted as holy people along with their Muslim saints. Sufism advocated looking inward, working on your own soul, fighting the inner battles — *jihad an-nafs* — the war of the soul — which rage inside the human being. It looked upon politics, or any efforts to change the environment and society, with disdain. Change yourself, transform your own life, and that will change the world.

Indeed great Sufis, such as Ibn Arabi, expressed solidarity with others — even other religions — who were working on their own souls as well. Together, though differently, all paths would reach God.

The Sufis' apolitical attitude worked well for the rulers of the medieval Muslim world who were generally not so pious even if they called themselves Muslim. But by the 20th century, with Western values of enlightenment seeping into the Islamic world, Sufism fell out of favor, and fundamentalism reared its evil head. Fundamentalism was also pious Islam, as Sufism was, but the difference was in interpreting where the pious work had to be done. Whereas Sufism emphasized working on yourself, fundamentalism looked back to the time of Muhammad, when he led the fledgling Islamic Ummah to victories against the surrounding tribes — including the Jewish tribes in Arabia. Fundamentalism was outward looking; it was a political animal. Never mind the inner struggles of the soul — outward piety would suffice. The true struggle was to reshape society, transform the world and eliminate any forces that might slow down this effort, or that might present to someone an alternative to the Islam of the days of Muhammad. For fundamentalism, what someone else is doing, someone else's status and identity, is essential: If you are not acting according to Islam, it affects me.

If you allow a society to offer anyone any other approach than what existed in seventh-century Medina and Mecca, you are harming my Islam. Therefore fundamentalism cannot tolerate a free society, or a democratic society — ruled by the tyranny of humankind rather than by God's laws — or certainly a society where other religions — Judaism or Christianity or Buddhism — are presented as legitimate alternatives to Islam. Everything in this world needs to be controlled, and a controlled Islamic society is the purpose of the world. Anyone opposed to this is the enemy, and eternal jihad is waged against this enemy.

The only humor in this is that fundamentalism is so intolerant, so interested in changing and eliminating the other, that frequently fundamentalists cannot tolerate each other. So, for instance, the Taliban regime, who are Sunni fundamentalists, see the Iranians — who may think they are religious but are of the Shi'ite sect — as heretics, and occasionally the Taliban pick fights with them. One of the things that frustrated me in my studies of Islamic fundamentalism was that because the fundamentalists cannot even agree on who they support and who is the greater enemy, understanding their philosophy will not really help in predicting their behavior. Some fundamentalists supported Saddam Hussein, a secular Muslim, against America, but others saw secular Islam as the greater threat and supported all efforts to drive out Hussein. Understanding Islamic fundamentalism might be far more helpful when we use that understanding as Jews to figure out who *we* really are.

Because here we are, on Kol Nidrei night. This is perhaps the moment of greatest commitment to God in our lives. And the question for all of us is, are we Sufis — looking inward at changing ourselves — or are we closer to the fundamentalist tradition — trying to change those around us. The answer, even before we have a chance to think about it, is: *Anu matirim l'hitpalel im ha'avaryanim*, "We remove all barriers that might cast judgment against others." The environment we want on Yom Kippur is one of tolerance and acceptance — yes, even validation for everyone who has come to daven here. And this is at the moment when we feel holiest and closest to God.

The law is clear; it is in your *machzorim* as well in the Talmudic footnote by Phillip Birnbaum, "When fasts and public prayers are conducted, the good and the bad must come together, united." Judaism does not deny human nature, the tendency to look around and note, "Oh, this person did this awful thing," or, "This person did something I would never do," or even "I am the worst person in the world because I do such and such." But our tradition takes a strong stand and demands that everyone be accepted. Not only accepted, but necessary: From tractate *Kritot* (dealing with serious punishments): "Any public fast that does not include the worst sinners of Israel, is not really a fast at all, [it is a charade]." We want everyone here. We need everyone here. And we don't want everyone here living their lives as we do, being just like us. We want them here as they are, working and struggling, fasting and praying to the best of their abilities, validated for who they are.

The beautiful source for this inclusiveness is the galbanum in the eleven spices used in the Temple. To put it bluntly, although the galbanum stunk, it was a necessary part of the incense formula — in equal portion to the frankincense, cloves, and balms among other spices. In fact the rabbis say that if you left out any one of the spices — the pious sweet-smelling ones or the galbanum — you would be subject to the death penalty. There was to be no whitewashing of the community; each person had his or her own flavor and smell and they all had to contribute that flavor and smell for society to function.

What our rabbis were advocating, by interpreting the Torah's ritual spices, was a society made up not of individuals trying to change each other, but individuals working together — at their own pace and in their own styles, to change themselves. Each person working on his or her own soul, waging *jihad an-nafs* — the struggle of the soul. And the clove worked as hard as the galbanum — side by side, in amity and unity.

This is true every day of the year, every Shabbat and every festival. But it reached its peak expression on Yom Kippur. Then, as the Torah tells us in tomorrow's reading, the High Priest would enter the Holy of Holies, the only time of the year he was permitted to reach so close to the Divine presence. And what would surround him on that day? "He shall take a pan full of burning hot coals — there is the piety and fervor! — and fill his hands with the fragrant incense, finely ground, and bring it inside the curtain. He shall put the incense of the fire before the Lord so that the cloud of the incense may be all over the cover of the Ark, otherwise he shall die." The *midrash* on these verses says, "The incense comes from the entire public, not just from the righteous few. And every spice must be in it — including the galbanum!"

What if our community wants to greet God without the foul-smelling galbanum? It will be the death of our community! When we go before God, we go with all of Israel around us. We want to be praying, fasting, and celebrating our relationship with God with everyone — good and bad. We are forbidden to ever try to change the eleven ingredients of the *k'toret* — just as our path in society is not to focus on uprooting evil and sinners. Our battle is to bring us back to God, and we have all the other ten spices — all those around us — to help us in our individual journeys to find God.

It shouldn't be too difficult to understand, then, why I gave up studying about Muslim fundamentalists, to join a community like Anshe Sholom. Every moment that Anshe Sholom is open, we strive to recreate the atmosphere of the incense — offered every day, but wafting throughout the

Holy of Holies only on Yom Kippur. Anshe Sholom is a community that accepts everyone who cares about Judaism and our tradition. Where they find themselves in observance, or commitment, or piety, or compliance is an individual struggle. Our dream at Anshe Sholom is not to have a community of *tzadikim* but to have all eleven spices entering our doors, learning together, singing together, sharing Shabbat dinners and lunches and walks together. All eleven spices having their kids play together, or helping those less fortunate in society — the hungry and the needy — together. All the spices are engaged in their own personal struggles to grow, learn more, find out what God and their souls want of them. This synagogue strives to be a place where they can all come, together, to be individuals but to enjoy their fellow spices. May our *k'toret* — our sweet-smelling, pungent, but beautiful cloud of incense — usher in a year when intolerance is obliterated from our world, and our community sets the model where piety and individual struggle ensure acceptance of the struggles of others.

"*Viyhi no'am Hashem aleinu.*" May God bless us for our hard work transforming ourselves, with a final sealing for a good and sweet New Year and a world around us filled with peace and respect for one another.

Rabbi Asher Lopatin is the Spiritual Director of Anshe Sholom B'nai Israel Congregation in Chicago, a Modern Orthodox synagogue. He is a former Rhodes Scholar and Wexner Graduate Fellow, and a student of Rabbi Aaron Soloveichik.

Reaching the Opposite Shore

Barbara Penzner

*Knowing that we have an appointed time to
mourn the dead, we can reenter life.*

These past few days, reeling from the events of
September 11, I have been feeling adrift, as if I were
alone in a rowboat just offshore, unable to return to
where I started, but feeling too far away from the opposite
shore. My boat rides the current as I watch the images and
hear the reactions, and sometimes I find the strength to row
a little, sometimes I get a better sense of where I'm going. But
I do not yet have the strength, or the current, or the wind
behind me, to reach the opposite shore.

Every once in a while, I hear a call for us to "move on with
our lives." Some have said that Americans have too short a
memory, and are not able to absorb events deeply and fully.
I am also aware that many, many people are not ready to
"move on."

What we are all experiencing, on many levels and for

many reasons, is grief. My little boat has no direction; I need to stop rowing long enough to grieve the brutal and violent deaths of thousands of innocent people. I grieve for the people of New York, whose horizon, forever changed, will trigger a regular reliving of their loss and pain. I grieve for our loss of innocence and security as a nation, and for the potential loss of liberty that comes with increased security. I grieve for our world, which may never rid itself of terror, or war, or violence. I grieve for the uncertainty of these days and for the awareness that there may be more grief to come.

Rachel Naomi Remen's book *My Grandfather's Blessings* has been a source of inspiration these past few weeks as I have pondered the awesomeness of life in preparation for these holy days. She teaches the following about the importance of living with grief:

"Grieving is the way that loss can heal. Yet many people do not know how to grieve and heal their losses. This makes it hard to find the courage to participate fully in life. At some deep level, it may make us unwilling to be openhearted or present, to become attached or intimate. We trust our bodies to heal because of the gift of a billion years of biological evolution. But how might you live if you did not know that your body could heal? Would you ride your bike, drive a car, use a knife to cut up your dinner? Or would you never get off the couch? Many people have become emotional couch potatoes because they do not know that they can heal their hearts.

"Unless we learn to grieve we may need to live life at a distance in order to protect ourselves from pain. We may not be able to risk having anything that really matters to us or allow ourselves to be touched, to be intimate, to care or be cared about. Untouched, we will suffer anyway. We just will not be transformed by our suffering. Grieving may be one of the most fundamental of life skills. It is the way that the heart can heal from loss and go on to love again and grow wise."

As I have listened to the testimonials and connected with friends far and near, I have encountered everyone at a different stage in their grief. Each person's stage dictates how he or she is responding to this traumatic event. On the first day, many parents responded by running home, rushing to pull children out of school, keeping everyone together and safe. By the weekend, while some were lighting candles, others were raising flags.

Thirty years ago, Elisabeth Kubler-Ross's book *On Death and Dying* introduced us to the notion of the five stages of grief: denial and isolation, anger, bargaining, depression, and acceptance. Each of us responds according to our stage of grief.

In the Torah portion *V'zot Habracha*, we read and spoke about the obligation to choose life. The operative phrase is to choose, taking the time to measure our response. Being human, in Jewish tradition, is to understand that we have choices. We have the choice of good over evil, and an awareness to recognize the difference between them. As God's creatures, created *b'tzelem Elohim* — in God's image — each of us carries within a fragment of the Divine. Therefore, even as we acknowledge the natural progression of grief, we know that there are multiple ways of acting on this grief.

This is a time of reaching opposite conclusions. When the world is turned on its head, we need to stand on our hands rather than our feet. We cannot return to where we came from, so we must seek to reach the opposite shore.

In my little drifting boat, the wave of denial and isolation hits first. Should I hold my children near, should our country protect our own and forget about the rest of the world? Or can we be brave enough to reach the opposite conclusion, to look every human being in the eye and recognize our common vulnerability?

Psalm 27 is recited at every service since this season of repentance began a month ago. This psalm offers ancient words of wisdom for responding to grief. While we might find little solace in words like "on the day of trouble God will shield me, lifting me to safety," we can find peace in its assurance of God's presence in time of pain, with its opening lines:

"The Lord is my light and my help, whom shall I fear?

The Lord is the strength of my life, whom shall I dread?"

Next in my little boat comes the wave of anger. Anger feeds vengeance, and vengeance reignites the cycle of violence. Can we take our anger and use it to feed justice? Rather than attack other nations indiscriminately, or target people because of their facial features or dress, or even blame the authorities that "let this happen," can we redirect our anger? Can we renounce hateful violence?

Wendell Berry has written:

"We are disposed, somewhat by culture and somewhat by nature, to solve our problems by violence, and even to enjoy doing so. And yet by now all of us must at least have suspected that our right to live, to be free, and to be at peace is not guaranteed by any act of violence. It can be guaranteed only by our willingness that all other persons should live, be free, and be at peace."

Psalm 27 continues, echoing his thoughts:
"O Lord, turn not in anger from Your servant.
Teach me Your way, O Lord; lead me on a straight path.
Deliver me not to the will of my enemies."

The next wave to rock my boat is bargaining. What can we do to mitigate this disaster? What can we give in return? Sometimes, however, we are too quick to give away what is dear. One of the airport security workers was quoted in the newspaper saying she would give her own life if she could have stopped the hijackers. But there is no bargain to be made; there is no changing the past. The response to bargaining is giving whatever we can, without expectation of reward: the brave rescuers who risked and lost their own lives, the droves of people across the country who waited in line to donate blood, the compassionate ones who arrived to heal the sick and comfort the mourners.

The psalm then offers up this prayer:
"O Lord, hear my voice when I call
Be gracious to me and answer me."

The boat hits a larger wave — depression. How do we move forward? What kind of a world are we bequeathing to our children? How can anyone know joy again? But of course, we have heard over and over again that the best way to resist terror is defiantly and joyfully to choose life. All has not been lost, unless we forget to be grateful for what we have. We need the courage to face a world that has been shaken and work to make it safe once again.

The psalm continues:
"In God's Tabernacle I will bring offerings of jubilation,
With chanting and joyous singing."

And finally, acceptance comes because we have not lost

hope. We cannot reach acceptance without knowing the other stages; healing itself is a response to pain and suffering.

Psalm 27 puts it,

> "Trust in the Lord and be strong:
> Take courage and hope in the Lord."

Only by facing our fears, by sharing our grief, can we reach acceptance and move on. Having survived the waves in our little boat, we will reach the opposite shore:

> "One thing I ask of the Lord, for this do I yearn
> That I may dwell in the house of the Lord all my life,
> To feel the goodness of the Lord in the Lord's sanctuary."

The background noise of the news will eventually fade, and the foghorn of alarm in our minds will soften. The gaping wound in the social landscape of our nation will take much longer to heal, and scars will remain charred in the ground and seared in our memories.

Acceptance does not mean forgetting. Acceptance itself is a religious struggle, a balancing act between compassion and conviction. We feel sorrow and will continue to feel it for some time. Each day we should carve out time to acknowledge this tragedy. Take three hours or five minutes to devote to your sorrow. As time passes, the time you need will likely diminish, although the sorrow may never entirely disappear. In that dedicated time we can honor the memories, show compassion to the survivors, and stand in reverence before this enormous evil.

We cannot dwell in this shock or pain, lest we succumb to living in despair and fear. Mourners will tell you how important it is for them to say *kaddish* for loved ones each day for eleven months. Knowing that they have an appointed time to remember the dead, they can reenter life. Having committed that time, we need to turn the page and allow ourselves to go on with our lives.

This is the value of ritual, of falling back on a secure structure for our emotions in times of confusion and anxiety. At the New Year, we are fortunate to have symbols and rituals to carry us across the choppy waters. The most poignant symbol acknowledging our acceptance of God's power and defiance of terror is the *sukkah*.

The *sukkah* is our concrete demonstration that, though our sense of safety has been blasted to bits, our only true security comes from God. If the terrorists chose the Twin Towers as a symbol of American wealth and power, we choose to dedicate our *sukkah* to the values of simplicity and community. I urge everyone here to find a way to build a *sukkah* this year. If you find that impossible, then arrange to eat at least one meal in a *sukkah*. Invite each other to your *sukkah*, come share meals in the Temple's *sukkah*. Use it as a gathering place for transforming our world into a place where violence cannot rule and where justice must prevail.

Because after acceptance, there is one more stage, a stage that Kubler-Ross does not document. That is the stage of *tikkun*, of repair. We cannot repair the broken lives, but we can work to ensure that our world does not foster hatred or terror, does not allow evil to triumph, and does not measure success in material terms alone.

The musicians among us will write beautiful music, and the artists will create profound works of art. The writers will string words together to express what we have been unable to say. Parents will give children loving embraces, and children will offer us their innocent awareness. The peacemakers will work to bring bitter enemies to sit together. The engineers will discover new ways to make our world at least seem a bit safer.

We will all feel more empathy with individuals who live with terror throughout the world, but especially with our brothers and sisters in Israel, who can teach us how life continues in the face of adversity.

The days ahead demand that we refrain from jumping too quickly to conclusions, but they also demand that we avoid becoming paralyzed. I close with a poem chosen by Kubler-Ross to open her book. The poem, "Fruit-Gathering," is by the Indian poet Rabindranath Tagore.

"Let me not pray to be sheltered from dangers but to be fearless in facing them.

Let me not beg for the stilling of my pain but for the heart to conquer it.

Let me not look for allies in life's battlefield but to my own strength.

Let me not crave in anxious fear to be saved but hope for the patience to win my freedom.

Grant me that I may not be a coward, feeling your mercy in my success alone; but let me find the grasp of your hand in my failure."

Rabbi Barbara Penzner serves Temple Hillel B'nai Torah in West Roxbury, Massachusetts. Before coming to Hillel B'nai Torah, she spent two years with her family studying in Israel as a Jerusalem Fellow. Rabbi Penzner is a past President of the Reconstructionist Rabbinical Association. She and her husband, Brian Rosman, have two children.

Enduring Unspeakable Loss

Carl M. Perkins

Unetaneh Tokef *teaches us how, in a world
of uncertainty and suffering, we should
respond to our existing reality.*

Tuesday, September 11, began like any other day. Some of us woke up on our own; others had to be nudged out of sleep. We washed, we dressed; we went off to work, or to school; we may have gotten kids off to school. But then, within a few minutes, the focus of our day shifted dramatically. Whatever we may have been concentrating on, whatever may have held our attention, soon shifted to the periphery. We entered a new reality, filled with *khil u'readah*, fear and trembling.

In our High Holiday liturgy, there is a prayer that attempts to capture that feeling: the *Unetaneh Tokef*. No matter what stage of life or state of mind, the *Unetaneh Tokef* stops us short. This year, it seems eerily and extraordinarily contemporary as it describes, in excruciating detail, the fragility of life and the utter unpredictability of our future.

On Rosh Hashanah it is written and on Yom Kippur it
is sealed:
Who shall live, and who shall die;
Who shall live out his days, and who shall not;
Who shall perish by fire, and who by water;
Who by the sword, who by a wild beast;
Who by hunger, and who by thirst;
Who by the ground trembling beneath him, and who by
illness;
Who shall be at rest and who shall be tormented;
Who shall be wealthy and who impoverished;
Who shall be humbled and who shall be exalted. ...

The misery described in that prayer is truly horrific. In an
ordinary year, most of us, when we recite the *Unetaneh Tokef*,
may focus on the unpredictability of life, but we probably
don't give much attention to the possibility that we might
suffer, or lose our lives, at the hands of another. After all,
how likely is it that we, living our comfortable lives in
America, would become victims of violence?

This year is very different. This year, even before getting
to the *Unetaneh Tokef*, all of us are wondering just that.

Unetaneh Tokef is not a new prayer. A 12th-century manuscript by Rabbi Ephraim ben Jacob of Bonn tells us how,
according to legend, Rabbi Amnon of Mainz, who lived just
before the Crusades, came to compose the *Unetaneh Tokef*
prayer. I never before felt it appropriate to share this legend,
but this year I feel differently. Here is what the manuscript
says:

Rabbi Amnon of Mainz was one of the great men of his
generation. He was handsome, wealthy, and well esteemed.
The local ruler, the Archbishop of Mainz, kept insisting that

he abandon his faith. He repeatedly refused. Finally, he said he needed three days to consider the matter. But once he left his presence, he felt enormous remorse, since he had let it be believed that he would even consider abandoning his faith. When he was sent for, he refused to go, so he was brought against his will to the ruler, who demanded to know why he had not come on his own. Amnon told him why and said, "I shall pronounce my own sentence. Let the tongue that spoke and lied to you, be cut off." The archbishop refused and said, "No, the tongue I shall not cut off, for it spoke well. But the feet that did not come to me at the time you set I shall lop off, and I shall torment the rest of your body as well."

Rosh Hashanah arrived. Rabbi Amnon asked his relatives to carry him to the synagogue just as he was and to lay him down near the *bima*. And it came to pass, as the cantor came to recite the *kedushah*, the "Sanctification," Rabbi Amnon said to him, "Stop: Let me sanctify the great name of God." And he cried out in a loud voice, "*uvchen l'cha taaleh kedushah*, May our sanctification ascend to you!" at which point he spontaneously composed and chanted *Unetaneh Tokef*. When he concluded it, his own end came, and he vanished from the earth before the eyes of all.

That legend reminds us that Jews have been exposed to unspeakable cruelty throughout our history, often perpetrated in the name of religion, and we've carried the memory of that horror with us. That legend is 900 years old. For hundreds of years before that, our people told stories of violence and bloodshed perpetrated against them, memories of what used to be called "man's inhumanity to man." To us, then, it should be no surprise that there is evil in the world and that there are people bent on afflicting other human beings.

Throughout history, we have repeatedly faced uncertainty, insecurity, and danger.

For many of us, however, confronting raw evil is a novelty. America has always seemed like such a safe country. What are we supposed to do?

We will long be reacting to the horror, the enormity of what we witnessed on September 11. What does our tradition suggest as a response to tragedy? Let us look at the text of *Unetaneh Tokef*, which provides Rabbi Amnon's answer. After presenting that horrible list of all the things that can happen to us, the text continues: "But *t'shuvah, tefillah*, and *tzedakah maavirin et roa hagezerah* — *T'shuvah*, repentance, *t'fillah*, prayer, and *tzedakah*, acts of lovingkindness, annul the severity of the decree."

This is a powerful assertion, but note what it does and does not say. The Hebrew phrase *ma'avirin et roa hagezerah* does not imply that our actions can cancel a decree, can prevent a tragedy. There are two kinds of tragedies that can happen to us: natural and of human origin. Sadly, we Jews have come to understand that we have little control over either of them. God created the world to function according to the laws of nature, and God created human beings with the freedom to choose to do good or evil. And we must live with the consequences.

The focus of this prayer is not annulling any decree. Rather, it is to teach us how, in a world of uncertainty and suffering, we should respond to our existential reality. It assures us that the *roa hagezerah*, the severity of the decree, the pain and suffering that are intrinsic to life, can be diminished.

How can we possibly diminish our pain? Let's discuss

each of the responses presented in the *Unetaneh Tokef.*

T'shuvah, repentance, is a very natural response to catastrophe. *T'shuvah* means to turn or orient one's self. You can't turn 180 degrees unless and until you stop, and that's what happens in the wake of a catastrophe. A certain clarity can come to us.

A friend of mine lives and works in New York. Her co-worker got married just ten days ago. Last Tuesday morning, she and her new husband took a cab from their home in Queens to catch a flight from LaGuardia to Disney World for their honeymoon. As they were about to get on the flight, they began to learn about the hijackings. The entire airport closed down. They were told to retrieve their luggage and leave the airport. There were no buses or taxis, so the newlyweds picked up their suitcases and left the airport on foot. It was a bizarre scene; hundreds and hundreds of people walking along the Grand Central Parkway to get as far away from the airport as possible.

Gradually, they realized they had been spared. They simply walked for about 45 minutes to their home, where they spent their honeymoon. They were very happy to do that, even though just one day earlier, they wouldn't have considered it.

Last week, the newspapers began publishing the transcripts of some cell phone conversations of the hijacked airline passengers as well as people trapped on the upper stories of the World Trade Center towers. The most common phrase to show up in those conversations was "I love you."

I'm sure that many of us have been kissing and hugging and saying "I love you" to our loved ones a lot more frequently since September 11.

We shouldn't need such terrible reminders to say "I love you." We shouldn't need such reminders to be *smeichim b'helkeinu*, happy with our lot, and to be real, present, and honest — to be men and women of integrity, to live our lives the way we know we should.

We should ask ourselves more often: How good are we, really, in doing what we should be doing? How *menschlich* are we? How effectively do we teach others to be *menschlich*? These questions are the foundation of *t'shuvah*. If we can ask them honestly we can accomplish much.

Another Jewish response is *tefillah*. We need prayer now more than ever. Not so much petitionary prayers, but what Rabbi Abraham Joshua Heschel calls prayers of empathy, prayers that help us determine what to pray for. That is why so many of us gathered after the attack for a candlelight vigil. The power of the holy word, the power of silent contemplation, the power of community — we feel these now more strongly than ever.

Finally, there is *tzedakah*. Last Tuesday, I visited the home of a woman in our community whose husband had boarded Flight 11 out of Boston but who did not live to reach his destination. It was a scene of shock and pain and tears. But it was also a scene of great compassion. One neighbor was taking responsibility for the now fatherless children; another for providing food in the home. Still another was handling visitors. People were coming together, at the worst possible time, for someone in need. This is *tzedakah*, righteousness, in one of its highest forms.

The scene I witnessed was repeated in thousands of homes, across this nation, as people came together to help those who'd been affected most personally and deeply by this tragedy. Sometimes it isn't until after a tragedy that one realizes the enormous compassion and caring people are capable of. Sometimes it isn't until after a tragedy that we realize what we are capable of.

Think about that awful legend concerning the creation of *Unetaneh Tokef*. Think about how Amnon could have responded to his awful experience. Though we have been exposed to unspeakable cruelty throughout history, we have tried not to allow that memory to degrade us, embitter us, turn us away from the values that unite us — turn us into intolerant and merciless killers. Instead, we transformed that memory into something remarkably positive: desire to bring justice and mercy to the world.

I hope and pray that the same will be so here in America. America was founded on a beautiful dream. The dream is freedom and the equality of all human beings — democracy. Although America isn't perfect, it's a remarkably humane country founded on an enlightened ideal we all can and should appreciate. While we have been dealt a painful blow, I hope that we never abandon the "noble ideals and free institutions that are our country's glory."

Having been exposed to many disturbing, even horrifying images during the past week, I want to close with one more redemptive.

On September 12, at the synagogue in the middle of the afternoon, we organized two separate assemblies for our religious school students, to help them cope with their feelings in the wake of the attacks and to help them appreciate Jewish responses to the tragedy. It was unpleasant to share with children the sadness of the hour.

At one point, I stepped outside for some air, and what I

saw was a sight for sore eyes. There, in the back of our property, just past the school wing, were two members of our congregation putting up the frame of our communal *sukkah*. I was never happier to see a *sukkah*. It never looked more beautiful, more precious, more impressive.

On the day after witnessing the collapse of two of the tallest, most secure and firmly constructed buildings in the world, we put up an intentionally temporary and fragile *sukkah*. What a contrast! What a sign of hope! The *sukkah*, on the one hand, symbolizes our vulnerability, our fragile world. Physical protection will always be chancy. But when we look up at the *skhach*, and through it to the sky, we are reminded of God's sheltering presence. As ephemeral as that is, we pray to feel it even when we're feeling most vulnerable. The *sukkah* represents our faith, our hope, our commitment to living a joyful life — even in the face of hardship.

Mahatma Gandhi once said, "When I despair, I remember that all through history the ways of truth and love have always won. There have been tyrants and murderers, and for a time they may seem invincible, but in the end they always fall. Think of it…: always."

May his words continue to be true. *Keyn y'hi ratzon.* So may it be God's will. Amen.

Rabbi Carl Perkins is Spiritual Leader of Temple Aliyah in Needham, MA. Before pursuing the rabbinate, he earned his law degree at Harvard and practiced law for several years in Boston. Rabbi Perkins was awarded a Wexner Fellowship to pursue rabbinical studies at the Jewish Theological Seminary of America. He authored the recently revised edition of Embracing Judaism, *written by his late father-in-law, Rabbi Simcha Kling.*

A Knife in the Heart

Joel Sisenwine

Today, I read the the binding of Isaac with terror.

Today, as we conclude a horrifying week, we read a biblical tale of terror: the binding of Isaac. "There came a time when God put Abraham to the test. 'Abraham!,' God said, and Abraham answered: '*Hineni*, Here I am.' God said: 'Take your son, your precious one, Isaac, whom you love, and go to the land of Moriah, and offer him up as a burnt offering on one of the hills that I will show you.' Early next morning, Abraham heeded God's command. He saddled his donkey, took his two servants, along with his son Isaac, and set out for the place as God had told him. On the third day, Abraham looked up, saw the place from afar, and said to his servants: "Stay here with the donkey while the boy and I go up to serve God" ["the boy and I" — Abraham couldn't even mention Isaac's name!].

Abraham took wood for the sacrifice and laid it on Isaac.

134

The biblical author now inserts the name and the relation-ship, to show how truly awful this is. "Abraham carried the fire stone and the knife; and the two walked on together."

Then Isaac broke the silence, with what today I consider to be the most significant line in the entire text.   Isaac asks a question that defines terror when he says, "Father! I see the fire stone and the wood; but where is the lamb for the burnt offering?"   He is asking, "What's happening here?   Am I next?!" That is to live in terror.

Abraham replies: "God will see to the lamb for the burnt offering, my son." They arrived at the place where God had told him and Abraham built an altar and carefully stacked the wood. He tied up his son, Isaac, laid him down, and reached for the knife to slay him.

"Father, where is the lamb for the burnt offering?!"

But the knife kept descending toward him, the knife — I imagine a little four-inch knife, a knife that could fit into a modern-day shaving kit — quickly piercing the air until an angel of the Lord called to him and said: "'Abraham, Abraham! Do not raise your hand against the boy, nor do the least thing to him ... for now I know you stand in awe of God' ... And Abraham looked up, and his eye fell upon a ram." There is the ram for the burnt offering. And he offered it in place of his son."

This year, the binding of Isaac sends chills down my spine. Sure, many will read the passage proudly and assert, "You see, in Judaism, God does not want human sacrifice. Life is sacred and should never be destroyed." But today, I read the tale in terror, like the rabbi who read it and broke down cry-ing. A small child came up to him and said, "Rabbi, Rabbi, why are you crying? You know that Isaac wasn't killed.

Angels came, they saved the day. Rabbi, angels don't come late." And the Rabbi replied, "I know my son, angels don't come late. But people do."

This week, everything seemed to come too late. And so, we questioned, "How could this happen?" Where is the ram for the burnt offering?

Chaim Gouri, an Israeli poet, wrote of the *Akeda* years ago. It resonates as though it were written yesterday. The poem is called "*Yerushah*," "Heritage," and it reads:

"The ram came last of all.

And Abraham did not know that it came to answer the boy's question — first of his strength when his day was on the wane.

The old man raised his head.

Seeing that it was no dream and that the angel stood there — the knife slipped from his hand..."

It continues, "Isaac, as the story goes, was not sacrificed.

He lived for many years, saw what pleasure had to offer, until his eyesight dimmed.

But he bequeathed that hour to his offspring.

They are born with a knife in their hearts."

You see, Isaac didn't get away unharmed. The knife slipped! It slipped from Abraham's hand and entered Isaac's heart and every person after him. And on September 11, we felt it. That knife, that four-inch knife, pierced our hearts, and stayed there.

"Rabbi, a plane just hit the World Trade Center. You better come watch."

"Rabbi, a second plane; it's horrible; it just hit the other tower."

The news spread as fast as the knife sliced through the air.

All U.S. airports, closed. Amtrak, Boston to Washington corridor, closed. All museums and monuments in Washington, D.C., closed. The Mall of America, closed. Disney World, closed. America, as we knew it, closed.

How do we live in a time of terror, with a knife lodged deep in our hearts? How do we go on, not knowing when the next bomb will blast? Let's look at Isaac, the first person I know who had a knife in his heart. If you look at the Torah, we're never told where Isaac goes after the binding. He suddenly appears a few chapters later, with no mention of his post-trauma whereabouts. The rabbis filled in the missing pieces in *midrash*, when they said that Isaac, following the *Akeda*, went to a yeshiva ... to think, reflect, and try to learn about God, life, and how to live with a knife permanently stuck in one's heart. And even though Isaac is wounded, he studies, and even though he studies, he's wounded.

Tuesday, the calls came in with the poignant questions: "Rabbi, I am petrified. I'm taking my child from school. How can I send him?"

"Rabbi, I'm not going back to work, especially in that high-rise building."

"Rabbi, I'm never flying again."

I'm sure Isaac felt the same way; he had a knife in his heart. But eventually, Isaac is told to get on with life, take a wife and go on living. But he wasn't ready.

"Find him a wife," his servants are told. "Find him the most 'beautiful,' most wonderful maiden in the entire land." And, according to Torah, they did. Her name was Rebecca. She was beautiful, the Torah says, a rare adjective in the holy text. The two of them are brought together. Rebecca looks up ... and sees Isaac. Isaac looks up ... and he sees camels. It just wasn't time. There was a knife in his heart.

Recently, a local woman passed away. In 1942, she survived the deadly Coconut Grove fire in Boston, where many people perished. For the last 59 years, she never entered a public building. That's no way to live.

And so Isaac's servants told him to live. Finally, Isaac brought Rebecca into his tent, took her as his wife, and, as the Torah says, "loved her." Finally, he was able to live again. And only a few verses after the *Akeda*, Isaac makes the greatest statement of faith when he says, "God grant me a child."

Isaac's approach to life is the exact opposite of the terrorist's approach. The terrorist believes that life is valueless. You can destroy everything, including yourself.

In Judaism, we're told to choose life. *U'vcharta b'chaim*, we read on Yom Kippur. "Choose life" because the world is still good, despite the knife that rests in our hearts.

We have to choose life ... and continue to affirm that the world is still good. And that people are too.

There was once a teacher who asked her students to list the names of the other students in the room on two sheets of paper, leaving a space between each name. She then told them to think of the nicest thing they could say about each of their classmates ... and write it down. It took the remainder of the class period to finish the assignment. As the students left the room, they handed in the papers. That Saturday, the teacher wrote down the name of each student on a separate sheet of paper and listed what everyone else had said about that individual. On Monday, she gave each student his or her list. Before long, the entire class was smiling. "Really?" she heard whispered. "I never knew that I meant anything to anyone!" "I didn't know others liked me so much."

No one ever mentioned those papers in class again. The teacher never knew if they discussed them after class or with their parents; it didn't matter. The exercise had accomplished its purpose. The students were happy with themselves and one another.

That group of students moved on. Several years later, one of the students was killed in Vietnam and his teacher attended the funeral. She had never seen a serviceman in a military coffin before. He looked so handsome, so mature. The church was packed with his friends. One by one, those who loved him took a last walk by the coffin. The teacher was the last one to bless the coffin. As she stood there, one of the soldiers, who acted as pallbearer, came up to her. "Were you Mark's math teacher?" She nodded: "Yes."

"Mark talked about you a lot." After the funeral, most of Mark's former classmates went out to lunch. Mark's mother and father were there too, obviously waiting to speak with his teacher. "We want to show you something," his father said, taking a wallet out of his pocket. "They found this on Mark when he was killed. We thought you might recognize it."

Opening the billfold, he carefully removed two worn pieces of notepaper that had obviously been taped, folded and refolded many times. The teacher knew, without looking, that the papers had held the list of all the good things each of Mark's classmates had said about him.

"Thank you so much for doing that," Mark's mother said. "As you can see, Mark treasured it." All of Mark's former classmates started to gather around with stories about how they had saved their lists. One of the classmates reached into her pocketbook, took out her wallet, and showed her worn and frazzled list to the group. "I carry this with me at all times," she said. "I think we all saved our lists." That's when the teacher finally sat down and cried. She cried for Mark and for all his friends who would never see him again. She cried for the times when we don't tell people how good they are.

And so Isaac called his sons together. And he said, "I want to speak with you, I want to tell you how much you mean to me. I want to bless you." And Isaac, with a knife in his heart, offered blessing. "The world's still good and you are too. Go forth, my sons, go forth."

We are a resolute people. We have known pain and heartache, but we have also known how to care and love and live again. Following the Kennedy assassination, Mary McGrory said to Patrick Moynihan, "Oh Pat, we'll never laugh again." And Patrick Moynihan replied, "Mary, surely we'll laugh again. But we will never be young again." Recently, the Jewish columnist and social activist Leonard Fein commented that both were wrong. America laughed and America was young again. America will be strong, and one day, God willing, there will stand two big towers in the heart of Manhattan, calling out our commitment to love, to life, and to blessing.

Keyn y'hi ratzon. May it be God's will.

Joel Sisenwine is Senior Rabbi of Temple Beth Elohim of Wellesley, Massachusetts.

Are We Ready to Get Up from Shiva Yet?

Jeffrey Spitzer

As we stand to hear the call of the shofar, may it call out a freedom from terror and bigotry, a freedom that tolerates diversity and binds us together in common good.

A friend of ours, a congregationalist minister named Bill, used to joke that if the decision were based on how we deal with death, he'd convert to Judaism because our tradition is so insightful into the needs of the mourner. My father-in-law, after over 30 years in the pulpit, has said that only rarely has he seen a severe long-term psychological problem relating to grief in a mourner who has gone through the complete cycle of *shiva*, the seven days of mourning following the funeral, and *shloshim*, the 30 days of lesser mourning. And the converse, he asserts, is also true: every mourner he has dealt with who has had long-term psychological troubles had also shortened the prescribed time for mourning.

But with all of Judaism's wisdom about the process of mourning, one law never has made sense to me. According

141

to the laws of *avelut,* the laws of mourning, *shiva* ends when *Yomtov* starts — whether the person has mourned seven days or not. I remember many times on the day before *Yomtov* as I was decorating the *sukkah* or preparing for the seder, my wife, who is a rabbi, would go out to "get a family up from *shiva.*" Were they really ready to "get up"? Are we really ready to get up from *shiva* now?

As I came to shul this morning, the words *Shanah Tovah* (Happy New Year) caught in my throat because I know, as a mourner, I'm not supposed to exchange greetings. And I, personally, still feel like a mourner.

President Bush thinks we are ready. On Sunday he said, "Tomorrow when you get back to work, work hard like you always have." And Vice President Dick Cheney never seemed to take his mind off business in order to mourn; his hope for the nation was that "the American people would stick their thumb in the eye of the terrorists" and, basically, not sell their stock holdings.

Many millions of Americans have given blood and donated money to relief organizations; an equal number have gone to funerals, comforted mourners, lit candles and stood at vigils, prayed and hugged their children. I don't know if these millions are ready to get up from *shiva.* But we are not really getting up from *shiva* because so many of our dead lay unburied. We are not mourners after the funeral, but rather in a condition of *aninut* — that strange limbo between death and burial. Indeed, so many in our nation who wait to bury the missing are in that strange state of limbo, feeling unfaithful to the lost souls if they give up hope and acknowledge death, and yet knowing that these souls have been ripped from their arms by a tragedy of inconceivable proportions.

This, however, does not really solve our problem, because if Rosh Hashanah does not stop our mourning, will we get up from *shiva* come Yom Kippur, or Sukkot, or Shemini Atzeret? Will we, three weeks from now, be able to dance and sing with our usual abandon on Simchat Torah, as we rejoice in the regularity of the conclusion of one reading of the Torah and the beginning of another cycle?

We are not only mourning the loss of people; we are also facing anxieties about the possibility of the American military going into dangerous situations to seek vengeance and destroy the infrastructure of those who tried to destroy our freedom through terror. The crucial difference, then, is that we are not mourning as individuals but as an entire nation. When an individual gets up from *shiva*, she or he is surrounded by a community of nonmourners, a community of people for whom there was no break in the normal cycle of the calendar, a community of people who are mostly still intact, stable, and capable of providing ongoing comfort and support. But when the mourner is a nation, to whom can it turn for comfort when it gets up from *shiva*? The Talmud is full of stories of great rabbis mourning a child or a parent, and the difficulties of their students in trying to comfort them. So it is for us. When the nation that mourns is the leader of the free world, the nation that every other nation looks to for guidance, help, and support, to whom can we look for support when we get up from *shiva*?

The Jewish people, however, has been through this before. Ancient Jerusalem, like New York today, was both the cultural and economic center of the country and, like Washington, it was a political center as well. Of course, neither Washington nor New York suffered the kind of destruction that Jerusalem did, but the impact on our people, that is, on the American people, has been similar. How many of us have uttered the words "It will never be the same" during the past week?

After the destruction of Jerusalem, there were those who continued to mourn. A midrash (Tehillim 137) reports: "One should plaster one's entire home, and leave part unplastered as a memorial to Jerusalem..." What constitutes too little or too much mourning? I suggested to my family that this year we should not dip our apples in honey, but in salt. My daughter Gabriella responded quickly. "No, Abba, we need to dip our apples in honey even more this year, because we need the sweetness, because we are hoping for a sweet year." This is not just a self-serving response from a child with a sweet tooth; Gabriella is right. Dipping apples in honey is a prayer for the future, not a reflection of where we are right now. When we dip our apples in the honey and wish for a sweet year, we are praying with our food — and we need those prayers right now.

Even so, I am having a hard time saying Shanah Tovah. I looked to a Talmudic discussion about the time between the destruction of the first Temple in Jerusalem in 586 B.C.E. until the time of the so-called Great Assembly. In the Babylonian Talmud, Yoma 69b, R. Yehoshu'a ben Levi asked: "Why are the members of the Great Assembly called 'great'? 'Because they restored a crown to its former glory.' Moshe said, 'God, the great, mighty, and awesome.' *Ha-El, haGadol, haGibor, v'haNora*, and that formula became established in our Amidah."

Jeremiah [who lived through the destruction of the First Temple] came and said, "Non-Jews are dancing in the

Temple! Is God really awesome?" So he did not say "awesome." And when he prayed, he said *Ha-El, haGadol, v'haGibor* and left out *nora*.

"Daniel [who lived during the Babylonian exile] came and said, "Non-Jews are enslaving God's children. Where is God's might?" So he did not say "mighty." And when he prayed, he said *Ha-El, haGadol, v'haNora* and left out *gibor*.

"Along came [Nehemiah and the members of the Great Assembly] and they said, "To the contrary, this is God's might, that God conquers the negative impulse and shows patience with the wicked [who can repent]. And this is the awesomeness of God, for if there were not awe of the Holy Blessed One, how would one nation have been able to exist among all of the other nations?"

Basically, the members of the Great Assembly were great because they reinterpreted God's might and awe into theological terms that made sense of their experience. God is mighty in not punishing the wicked immediately, and allowing time for *t'shuvah*, repentance. God is awesome because the Jewish people still exists, and what could be better proof than that?

We can still rely on the reinterpretation of the Great Assembly. God doesn't intervene and still hopes for communal and individual repentance. Maybe it is awesome that, as the president has said, "America is back at work." But maybe it isn't Jewish tradition that needs reinterpreting this time. After the Holocaust, few of us ever express belief in a God who will intervene.

Perhaps what needs reinterpretation this time is our American tradition. How's this? The land of the free — that is to say, free enough to tolerate a diversity that includes those who would destroy that freedom — and the home of the brave — that is to say, brave enough to rebuild skyscrapers and board commercial jets.

Maybe we're not ready to reinterpret America's tradition. After all, the members of the Great Assembly weren't able to do their reinterpretation until the Temple was rebuilt. Maybe we need some time to reinterpret America in a way that makes sense. But in the meantime, I know that my eyes have seen a truth. And that brings me to the end of the passage of Talmud that I quoted. If we can just reinterpret ourselves out of our difficult theological crises, then why didn't Jeremiah and Daniel do just that? Why did they feel a need to change the words that Moshe had established? The Talmud asks:

"And [Jeremiah and Daniel], how could they do what they did and uproot the formula that Moshe established? Rabbi Elazar said: 'Since they knew that the Holy Blessed One is Truth, therefore, they could not lie.'"

Our eyes have also seen truths, and today, as we stand before the Holy Blessed One who is Truth, we cannot lie either. For some of us, the truth we see is the need to seek vengeance against those who have taken away so much from us. For some of us, the truth we see is the need to wipe out evil from our midst. For some of us, the truth we see is that democracy and the rule of law must take precedence even over our own security. And for some of us, the truth we see is to number our days, that we may get ourselves a heart of wisdom. Whatever truth we see, we do ourselves and our tradition a disservice when we lack the courage to take our tradition in our hands and adjust it to fit our circumstance, as did Jeremiah and Daniel.

In our home, we do an elaborate ritual on Rosh Hashanah

called *simanim*. Most of you probably do apples and honey for sweetness. Some of you might also do pomegranates for fruitfulness or productivity or a fish head to be at the head and not at the tail. In our family, we have a very long list of foods and puns that we make each year, like eating sugar cane and saying, "*Y'varekhekhah, Hashem, v'Yishmerekhah, keyn yehi ratzon,*" or before eating salad, "Please Lord, lettuce leaf our sins behind us." This year, I added one in English that reflects a truth I see: Each person takes a piece of celery or honey cake and recites: "May it be Your will O Lord, our God and God of our ancestors, that we may recognize that the ways of the Torah are peace, not that they lead to peace, but that they are peace, and may we create a world of peace through our actions."

This last Shabbat afternoon, as a group of adults and young people gathered around our table, it became clear that we all looked at the events of the last week through different eyes; we just saw different truths, and our discussion was not dispassionate. In hindsight, I am ready to give another shot at reinterpreting our American tradition.

The land of the free — where people of good conscience are free to express their opinions, even when they are unpopular, even when the need for unity is great — and the land of the brave — where people are brave enough to take necessary action for our national security, even when our grasp of the truth is somewhat less than God's own vision.

Ready or not, we are about to get up from *shiva*. We are about to get up and hear the shofar. As we stand and heed the call of the shofar, *t'ka b'shofar gadol l'heruteynu*, may it truly be a great shofar blast calling out our freedom and the freedom cherished by these United States, a freedom from terror and a freedom from bigotry, a freedom that tolerates diversity and a freedom that binds us together for our common good as one nation, under God, indivisible with liberty and justice for all of us.

———————

Jeffrey Spitzer is Producer of JSkyway (www.JSkyway.com), an online professional development project of Jewish Family & Life! for Jewish educators.

Unetaneh Tokef: The Spiritual Challenge of This Moment

Toba Spitzer

Will we, as a nation, respond out of anger and fear, or from a place of reason and clarity? Will our actions root out the potential for further violence or stoke the fires of hatred?

The words I'd like to share with you today come from the High Holiday liturgy, a prayer that is unique to Rosh Hashanah and Yom Kippur, called *Unetaneh Tokef*.

On the surface it's a difficult prayer, one which I know has turned off any number of Jews to synagogue worship. It seems to reflect a theology that is difficult if not impossible for most modern Jews to believe, a prayer addressed to a kind of "Santa Claus" god who records our deeds, sees who is naughty and who's nice, and then inscribes us for good or bad in the year to come.

This prayer, however, is more complicated than that. In language that might sound a bit foreign to our ears, *Unetaneh Tokef* attempts to get at a fundamental spiritual and existential truth that speaks to us every year — perhaps this year with more urgency.

It begins with a direct address to God, who is imagined as sitting on a throne: *v'yikon b'chesed kisecha*, a throne that is "established in love, in compassion." *V'teshev alav b'emet*, "and You sit upon it in truth." The power that we are called to experience on this holy day is a power that encompasses both truth, *emet*, and love, *chesed*. The next section reads: "True, you judge, you reprove, you intimately know, you write, you seal, you inscribe, you count, you remember all that is forgotten." Personally, I do not hold an image of God that encompasses these human actions. But this liturgy suggests that my actions affect, that they are "written," that quite literally, who I am and what I do "counts" in some profound way. This is made most clear in the final line of this section. We read, *v'chotem yad kol adam bo*. Literally, this means "The signature of every person is in it."

God, according to the prayer, may be the One who remembers and transcribes, but I am the author of my actions, and accountable for them.

A tension is addressed in the next segment of the prayer. How much is within our control? How much do we actually write, and how much is written for us?

In this next section, the imagery shifts, from God as judge on a throne, to the image of God as shepherd:

"And all who come into the world pass before You like sheep for the shepherd." This image seems to be based on a passage from the prophet Ezekiel (34:12), where God speaks of the people of Israel as a flock that has lost its shepherd. God must then seek them out and care for them. Echoing the language of Ezekiel, the prayer continues, *K'vakarat ro'eh edro, ma'avir tzono tachat shivto, ken ta'avir v'tispor v'timneh v'tifkod nefesh kol chai* ... "Like a shepherd who seeks out his flock, passing the herd under his staff, so do You make us pass by, and number, and take account of, and take notice of the spirit of every living being." This is not a judging image of God, but rather a loving one, the metaphor of a shepherd who knows intimately his or her flock, watching over each creature. We also see the power of the shepherd to decide the fate of the flock: "You decide for each creature its cycles of life, and you write down the destined decree."

And here begins the famous litany that seems to speak so powerfully of predestination: "On Rosh Hashanah it is written, and on Yom Kippur it is sealed: How many shall pass on, and how many shall thrive; who will live, and who will die, whose death is timely, and whose is not?"

Are these fates connected to our actions, to the statement in the beginning of the prayer that our deeds counted or recorded? Do we have any control over our fate, or are we truly as helpless as sheep?

The prayer itself raises this tension, as it goes on:

U't'shuvah, u'tefillah, u'tzedakah, ma'avirin et ro'ah ha'gezerah: But *t'shuvah* (turning), and *tefillah* (prayer), and *tzedakah* (acts of righteousness) transform or mitigate the harshness of the decree.

This section seems to first say, "We are sheep, we have no control, our destiny is sealed." The next lines speak directly to our own actions, our ability to change the destiny that's been decreed. Which is the true statement?

Let's look at the final section of the prayer, and then reflect on what all of this might mean for us.

"A human being's origin is in dust, and her end is dust; with her life she earns her bread. Like pottery, we break; like grass, we wither; like a flower, we fade; we are like a passing shadow, a dissipating cloud, a blowing wind, like scattered dust, like a dream that flies away."

This passage, the existential heart of *Unetaneh Tokef* prayer, poetically affirms the ephemeral nature of our lives as human beings. It states simply that our lives on this planet are limited. It is in the nature of this world that all living things come into being and then pass away. We are no different. This basic truth is unconnected to who we are, or what we do with our lives.

But the prayer does not end there. After this affirmation of the temporary nature of our own being, the liturgy declares, *V'atah hu melech el chai v'kayam*: But You are the Ultimate God, living and enduring.

Over against all of this impermanence, the constantly changing nature of all created things, is one true, Eternal Something, *El chai v'kayam*, the enduring power of Life itself. Of this Power we read, "There is no limit to Your years, no end to Your days, no measure to that which contains Your Presence, no way to comprehend Your name, Your essence."

This power stands in contrast to us, and yet we are intimately connected to It. The final words of the prayer are, *u'shmenu karata vishmecha*, Our name You have called in Your name." Our names, our essences, are somehow intimately related — both the name of ephemeral human life, and the name of godly eternity.

So. What is the *Unetaneh Tokef* about?

I would suggest that this prayer is not a statement of theology. It is a liturgical poem. It is a poet's attempt to capture a complicated truth about our existence.

We stand here, on Rosh Hashanah, aware of our mortality,

our vulnerability, the extent to which events in life are beyond our control. For some of us, this is an awareness that we have carried with us for months or years before any awareness borne of illness and death. For others, this awareness was driven into our hearts through the searing images from the TV on September 11. It is from this awareness that *Unetaneh Tokef* speaks to us.

And along with this awareness, the prayer affirms that against our own experience of vulnerability, there is something abiding, something eternal, something that serves to connect us in space as well as time.

The prayer speaks of a God who determines the life of each being, but also who awaits each person in forgiveness. I translate this into a less supernatural theology: There is a reality that includes events that are beyond our control as well as a reality that contains within it the possibility of transformation brought about by our actions. Both things are true; both are aspects of one reality. There is much that is beyond our control, but there is also an arena in which we do have power.

This possibility, this partnership, presents itself to us in this moment as a spiritual challenge.

We are standing at what feels like the edge of a crater. We can see, quite clearly, the limits of our human existence, the reality of our vulnerability and mortality. There is a certain assumption of "safety" that we need in order to function in our everyday lives, but in our deeper moments of truth, or in moments of crisis, whether personal or communal, we become aware of this reality. This is the truth of "like grass we wither, like flowers we fade, we are like scattered dust, like a dream that flies away." This awareness can be frightening, but it can also be liberating. This understanding, although we may achieve it in painful and difficult ways, is a most important awareness. It is our opportunity to live the fullest life possible in the days given to us. It is the ground of compassion, of being able to connect to others. It is, in a way that is at first hard to grasp, a true source of peace, a sense of wholeness.

In this awareness there is enormous potential for transformation. In this moment, in this place, we are given a way out of fear.

How, then, do we meet this spiritual challenge? By what means?

Unetaneh Tokef suggests three specific paths: *T'shuvah*, *tefillah*, and *tzedakah*.

T'shuvah: *T'shuvah* can be understood in a number of ways. Traditionally, it means "turning" or "returning" to God, to the godly path. It can also be understood as "return" to our own truest selves. In the morning blessings we say, *Elohai neshama sh'natatah bi tehorah hi* — my God, the soul you have placed in me is pure. In our essence, as human beings, we are pure. In the course of living our lives we can wander from that point of purity, we can take paths that diminish ourselves or that cause us to diminish others. *T'shuvah* is the opportunity to return, to remember and reclaim that point of goodness within. Rabbi Richard Hirsch translates *t'shuvah* as "direction." He writes, "*T'shuvah*, or turning-to-God/liness, is the process of deciding the direction of our lives" (*Kol Haneshamah Machzor*, p. 352). *T'shuvah* is about actions, our willingness to make changes that will allow us to lead lives that express the godly essence of our being.

T'shuvah can also be translated as "answer" or "response."

I cannot control all events that shape my life, but as long as I am alive, I have some measure of control over my *response* to those events. I can shape my actions, intentions, and the quality of my living.

In those moments, when we peer over the edge of that crater, we are given the opportunity for *t'shuvah*. What path have I been on? Is it the right path for me? What is the ultimate direction of my life? How can I be truest to myself, to the godliness within me? To what should I be listening, and how can I wisely respond to that voice? *T'shuvah* is about trusting the godliness in ourselves, about having faith in our own ability to respond.

Tefillah: Prayer. If *t'shuvah* is about connecting to something deep within ourselves, then we can understand *tefillah* as connecting to something beyond ourselves. *Tefillah* contains the challenge to realize that we are not the beginning and the end, that there is some Power beyond ourselves that calls to us, that waits for us, that is there to hold and comfort us. Through *tefillah* we are encouraged to look deeply within ourselves, to reflect on what holds ultimate meaning for us, and also to look beyond ourselves, to realize our place in the broader scheme of things.

We are also given this opportunity for connection in communal prayer where, although we may stand alone in our private hopes and needs, we stand together in a community that gives praise, seeks comfort, and joins voices in song and silence. What I would call God or godliness becomes quite palpable in moments such as these, when a group of individuals gather in order to reach beyond themselves and, in a community of *tefillah*, connect on many levels.

In moments of standing at the edge, when we feel alone in

the face of reality, we are given the gift and the challenge of *tefillah*. How am I connected not just to a godliness within myself, but to what lies outside of myself? How do I find the faith that there is something that awaits me, to which I can open my heart and my soul? What values will shape my life? *Tefillah* is about trust in a Power that lies beyond myself, about a willingness to suspend disbelief and let myself open to what surrounds me.

Tzedakah: *Simply* understood as giving financial support to those who are in need, it has a broader meaning. *Tzedakah* is how we connect to others, our responsibilities to those around us. The laws of *tzedakah* mandate that I recognize that the bounty I enjoy is not entirely of my own making; I am obligated to share with those in need. I do this out of the recognition that I too might one day be in need. *Tzedakah* teaches us that no one is self-sufficient, that we are bound in responsibility for one another.

When I come to the edge of the crater, when I realize my own vulnerability, when I experience suffering, I am connected in the most fundamental way to the rest of humanity. *Tzedakah* challenges me to open myself to people around me, in my immediate community or on the other side of the globe. It challenges me to acknowledge that what I think is "mine" is not entirely mine, that whatever I have been given is given on condition that I use it well. *Tzedakah* invites me to open my heart in generosity, and to experience my own well-being as the well-being of others.

So *t'shuvah*, *tefillah*, and *tzedakah* are ways that individuals can respond to the spiritual challenge of this moment. Each calls for connection to the godliness within ourselves and in the universe, to the people around us.

September 11 has forced a new awareness on us as Americans, an awareness that also presents a spiritual challenge. We are vulnerable. There is much to mourn.

T'shuvah and *tefillah*: Where do we turn? Where is the godliness in the violence of this past week? If the God of *Unetaneh Tokef* ordains who will live and who will die, how do we understand the suffering of thousands of innocent people?

We can't blame God for evil perpetrated by human beings. Jewish tradition understands God's creation as fundamentally good, yet because of the existence of free will, there is always the potential for human evil. Ungodly acts can occur in a godly universe. And the events of September 11 were most certainly ungodly.

Godliness lies in our potential to respond to events in such a way that God's presence is enhanced, not diminished further. The heroic efforts of those who risked their own lives to save others, the outpouring of support from people across the country and around the world, these are all sparks of godliness. But we are only at the beginning of the challenge this situation presents to us.

Much has been spoken in these past few days about the military and political challenges ahead, but I think the spiritual challenges are as great, if not greater.

T'shuvah, response. What will be our response? Will we, as a nation, respond out of anger and fear, or from a place of reason and clarity? Will our actions root out the potential for further violence, or will our actions only stoke the fires of hatred? Will we use the loss of our own innocents to justify taking the lives of others who are innocent? How can the words "collateral damage" even be spoken after a horror such as this?

Our vulnerability makes us fearful, but it is also an incredible opening. From suffering we learn compassion for others. Tens of millions of human beings around the globe are refugees, living daily with violence and the terror of gangs and governments. These are our brothers and sisters in suffering. Will we see ourselves in their faces, or will we try to rebuild the walls that have convinced us that we are somehow different?

As American Jews, we have been given a profound opportunity to create alliances with Muslim and Arab-Americans. Our shared scapegoating in this situation gives us the opportunity to forge real and lasting connections. Such an alliance could lead to dialogue and understanding, and, perhaps contribute to bringing peace in the Middle East.

Tzedakah: How do we express in material ways the underlying truth of interconnection? After our own country's healing has begun, once we have attended to those who have lost loved ones, or their livelihood, will we as a country be able to respond to the real roots of terrorism? Poverty and despair are the real enemies of peace and freedom. How will we fight them?

However dark the world might seem at this moment, the reality is that every new year, every new moment, holds hope and the potential of our response. Violence and suffering are not new. But our ability to transform violence into compassion, to bring peace from suffering, is a possibility held out to us. I'd like to end with a few words from Rabbi Ira Eisenstein, the son-in-law of Mordecai Kaplan, the founder of Reconstructionism. Rabbi Eisenstein was in many ways the person who built the Reconstructionist movement, and he died this past summer after living a long and inspiring life. In 1983, he wrote:

"For me, God is the name we attach to those powers in nature and in [humanity] which promote harmony and growth, interdependence and individualization ... I want to improve the world. The question is: can it be done, and how? The first question demands faith, that is, faith in the potency of that Power. Is the potential powerful enough to overcome the chaos of human nature? If the answer is yes, then the next item on the agenda is: how? What are the means available and how can those means be best utilized to achieve the desirable ends? Speculation concerning ultimate things is a pleasant occupation, but there is work to be done, and that work presupposes only one affirmation about the nature of life: namely, that the potential is there." ("Valedictory," *The Reconstructionist*, Summer 1983.)

Like Rabbi Eisenstein, I believe the potential is there. And I agree that there is work to be done. My sincere prayer for all of us is that we find our own way, through our own process of *t'shuvah*, *tefillah*, and *tzedakah*, through our own work of turning, reflecting, and connecting to others, to make that potential manifest in this new year. I pray for strength of spirit, compassion, wisdom, and clarity for all of us. May this be a year of healing and of expanded vision, a year when we meet the spiritual challenge set before us.

Rabbi Toba Spitzer is the Spiritual Leader of the Reconstructionist congregation Dorshei Tzedek in West Newton, Massachusetts.

Living Well in Our Dalet Amot (Our Personal Sphere of Influence)

Jeffrey A. Summit

A key to a family's recovery is having one person who holds and articulates a vision of hope.

I n the face of large events, such as the tragedies we experienced on September 11, there is a tendency for the individual to feel small and powerless. What can we do to make a difference? What can we do to alter or impact this history as it unfolds and shapes our lives? I see many people looking to our leaders for solace, direction, and guidance. And, in fact, it has been inspiring to see figures like Rudolph Guiliani epitomizing calm, vision, and leadership. Yet, on this Rosh Hashanah, I would like to suggest that while our leaders are important, life, as we live and experience it, is really shaped by each one of us in our daily actions and interactions.

I want to speak about the importance of living well within our own *dalet amot*, our personal sphere of influence, and what a profound difference that can make, both for us and to

160

the people we touch every day. I don't believe that we, as regular people, are powerless as large events unfold. In a very real way, we each have profound power to shape and influence the quality and experience of life in our world.

The basis for my observation comes from two directions. On the one hand, I am deeply influenced by the Jewish tradition's emphasis on the centrality of the individual in changing the world. *T'shuvah* (change, growth), in its essence, is the work of the empowered man or woman, making an individual decision that moves to action. While *t'shuvah* is supported by communal practice, such as fasting and public prayer, the hard work of personal change and growth is placed squarely in the lap of each man and woman. One of the essential messages of the *yamin noraim*, these days of awe, is that more than anything, each person's actions count.

The second influence is found in the writings of Benedict Anderson in his book *Imagined Communities: Reflections on the Origins and Spread of Nationalism* (1983), where he discusses a particular paradox of nationalism. While people have extremely strong feelings for nations, so strong that they will even fight and die for their country, the concept of a nation lives in our minds rather than in actual relationship with other individuals. Anderson explains that a nation, or even a large community such as "the Jewish community," is for the most part imagined because the members of even the smallest nation will never actually meet or know most of their fellow members. Yet in their minds lives the image of their community.

This concept helps me understand the student who comes to campus angry at the entire Jewish community because he had a mean Hebrew school teacher who yelled at him when he was in the seventh grade. Part of me wants to say, "Deal with it." Yet the student's personal experience with that one individual has shaped his imagined view of the Jewish community. So, I conclude, it is extremely important to pay attention to how we live in our small personal sphere. We are constantly contributing to the image of the community as constructed by those around us.

What does it look like for each of us to live through such a crisis as the terrorist attacks of September 11? I want to briefly suggest three areas for examination. First is the importance of being fully present in whatever place we inhabit. Next, I want to speak about embracing hope, and finally, I want to talk about why it is so important to assert the rock-solid Jewish belief that good eventually inches out evil in our world.

My first point is the incredible importance of being actively present in our lives. I think of the phrase in the Torah reading for the first day of Rosh Hashanah, "God heard the cry of Ishmael *ba'asher hu sham*," "in the place where he was" (Gen. 21:17). Why do these words strike me with such power? Perhaps because we have created technology that has challenged our ability to be fully present in any one place, at any one time. We can be called, beeped, faxed, emailed, and Fedexed anywhere. So much vies for our attention. We live in a world where we are both everywhere and nowhere.

To live well during a crisis such as this is being able to be fully present with the people around us. Being truly present with another human being is giving that person our full attention. It means looking into his or her eyes rather than over his or her shoulder at the TV. It is being willing to engage in thoughtful conversation at the dinner table even though you are exhausted. Being fully present is being comfortable to sit and be silent with a friend.

In truth, there is something worse than not being with the people we love. And that is to have them physically present but not really there. Joseph Soloveitchik's book *On Repentance* discusses "*ha'avodah sh'he balev*," "the service of the heart," and what it means to be fully present. Soloveitchik examines how Maimonides breaks prayer into two categories: the service of prayer, which like the service of the Temple consists of doing certain physical acts and saying certain words, and "*ha'avodah sh'he balev*," where "the heart must do its share" and "encompasses all of a person's being, joys and sorrows, grief as well as rejoicing" (p. 73). Soloveitchik stresses that the act of praying is merely the performance of the law, while the fulfillment of the law remains in the realm of the heart. So too, being fully present during difficult times like these requires both physical and emotional presence — if you care about people, it's important to show up. Once you are physically there, then it is essential to do that "heart work" and be emotionally involved and available.

Sometimes people are not present because they are uncertain of the words to say, or they fear they won't have the right answers to give. But being available in this crisis is not about knowing the right answers or what will happen next. It is certainly not about being able to explain the root causes of international terrorism. To a large extent, it is about being willing to make direct, focused, compassionate contact with the regular people who are part of our lives — our roommates, spouse, children, parents, the lady behind the cafeteria line, the guy next to you at the Post Office. Those are the interactions that shape the way we conceive of our communities, make us feel at ease or on edge, and build webs of connection in our daily lives.

Harold Kushner relates a story about a boy who tells his father that he is going over to help a friend who just broke his new bicycle. The father asks, "What do you know about fixing bicycles?" The son answers, "I don't know anything about fixing bicycles. I'm going over to help him cry." I think of people who have helped me when situations seemed dark. They did not flood me with wisdom, they did not magically fix things, and they were certainly not perfect. They were willing to spend time, talk, and listen. Sometimes their words even had a comforting cynicism, such as when Dick Israel, whose memory is a blessing, would say, "Things are rarely as bad or as good as they first appear." Never underestimate how important it is for you to be present, and hopeful, for those people directly around you.

That leads me to my second point, which is the importance of conveying hope. While many people have been singing "God Bless America," the song going through my head recently is *Hatikvah*, The Hope, Israel's national anthem. I was amused to read that, in an effort to teach Zionist values to young Israelis, Israel's broadcasting service was scrolling the lyrics of *Hatikvah* across the television screen; too few young people in Israel knew the words. Those words have much to teach us now. *Ode lo avdah tikvatenu, Hatikvah bat shanot alpayim.* We have not lost our hope, the hope that has persisted for thousands of years. The French poet Edmond Fleg wrote, "I am a Jew because where most people despair, the Jew hopes." In this era of instant gratification, it can be a profound gift to those around us to convey that it is possible to remain hopeful, even for a long time, before our goal is achieved.

I know from my rabbinic work with families in grief that a key to a family's recovery after experiencing tragedy is having one person in that family who holds and articulates a vision of hope. Many families will make it through a difficult time if just one person is able to look beyond to the other side of a crisis and to say that things will eventually be all right. Living well through this tragedy is being able to convey to the people around us, even in our fear and uncertainty, that our lives will go on and we will continue to work, love, play, and celebrate.

Finally, I want to speak about the importance of asserting a truth that we have learned over and over again as Jews. That truth is that good eventually inches out evil in our world. As Jews, we know that evil exists. That was not news on September 11. America may have been naïve. But we Jews are not naïve. We have looked evil in the face, and still we live today. We know how hard *t'shuvah* is, and yet every year, we insist that *t'shuvah* is possible. There will always be the haters but when we examine our history, we maintain that good will eventually triumph. Justice may not flow like a mighty stream and righteousness may not well up like great waters, but good will prevail. This is a powerful message, one that is at the core of our tradition, and why on both Rosh Hashanah and Yom Kippur we blow the long shofar note, *tekiah gedolah*, why we say *ha shana haba'a b'Yirushalayim*, next year in Jerusalem. I do not look at those words or actions as colorful rituals; I understand them to be expressions of the core values of my Judaism. *Af al pi sh'yitmamaya, ani ma'amin b'emunah sh'leimah*. Even though redemption is not yet here, I still fully and completely believe that good will eventually inch out evil. Living well in this difficult time is to accept and convey that truth. As Jews, I do not believe we have another option.

What you do now, how you live your life, can make a profound difference. I was struck by a letter that was recently sent to the *New York Times* by a student in high school after the World Trade Center went down. She writes, "I am a high school sophomore and I've been finding out what kind of people my friends are. One is fearful and has to be driven to and from school instead of taking the subway. Many are self-absorbed and narcissistic and their biggest worry is that certain people haven't called to check in on them." She describes another friend who was "so loving and caring" that she was completely incapacitated and all she could do was cry.

I feel bad for the high school students she describes, and I hope they find the courage and understanding to overcome their fears and self-centeredness. After all, that is one of the central messages of Rosh Hashanah and Yom Kippur — that change and growth are always possible.

You are probably all too familiar with the Rav Zusia story where Zusia says, "When I die, I'm not afraid that the Holy One is going to confront me and ask: 'Why weren't you Moshe Rabbenu?' I'm afraid God will ask me: 'Zusia, why weren't you Zusia?'" In these demanding times, that story doesn't quite cut it for me. I prefer the sharper edge conveyed by a rabbi I met when I was in high school who gave me clearer advice. He said, "Always be yourself. Unless, of course, you are an ass. In that case, be someone else."

These are demanding times, but we don't have to be superheroes or great national leaders to have an impact upon our immediate world. If we are able to be present for the people around us, remain hopeful and assert that good will eventually inch out evil in our world, each one of us can make a profound contribution. I wish for all of us the strength to live well during these difficult times.

———

Rabbi Jeffrey A. Summit is Director of the Hillel Foundation at Tufts University, where he is also Adjunct Associate Professor in the Department of Music. He is author of The Lord's Song in a Strange Land: Music and Identity in Contemporary Jewish Worship *(Oxford University Press, 2000). He is currently conducting research on the music and liturgical traditions of the Bayudaya (Jewish people) of Uganda.*

Contributors

Michael Balinsky
Michael Berenbaum
Saul Berman
Susan Berrin
Kathy Bloomfield
Alan Dershowitz
David Elcott
Reuven Firestone
Ronne Friedman
David Glanzberg-Krainin
Leila Gal Berner
Edwin Goldberg
Marc Gopin
Irving "Yitz" Greenberg
Sheryl Katz
William Lebeau
Asher Lopatin
Vanessa Ochs
Carl Perkins
Barbara Penzner
Arnold Resnicoff
Dawn Rose
Or Rose
Joel Sisenwine
Jeffrey Spitzer
Toba Spitzer
Jeffrey Summit
Dov Zakheim

Jewish Family & Life! Board of Directors

Martin Kaminer, *Chair*
Yosef I. Abramowitz
Michael Chartock
Jacob Ner-David
David Fishman
Hillel Levine
Evan Mendelson
David Mersky
Dan Perla
Michael Rukin
Rachel Sabath
Jeffrey Savit
Elie Wurtman

Honorary Board Members

Myra Kraft
Robert Malina
Elie Wiesel

WHAT DO YOU KNOW ABOUT *Sh'ma*?

Considered a pillar of modern Jewish thought for more than 30 years, the journal *Sh'ma* provides a monthly forum for cutting-edge Jewish issues that cross the social, religous, and political landscape. By offering a wide range of viewpoints within a sacred but sometimes heated conversation, *Sh'ma* serves as a public diary of the American Jewish experience.

Future *Sh'ma* issues will address such topics as Entering a Jewish-Muslim Dialogue, Hunger in the Jewish World, Young Writers on Judaism and Creativity, Jewish Identity among Secular Israelis, Where Is Rabbinic Education Headed?, Critical Decisions in Medical Ethics, Sacred Space, Trends in Jewish Scholarship, and Training Jewish Professional and Lay Leadership.

Says Brandeis University professor Jonathan D. Sarna, "*Sh'ma* offers more ideas per page than any other American Jewish periodical. In recent years, it has become must reading for anyone interested in the central issues facing American Jews."

SUBSCRIBE TODAY!
Information on the following page.

Sh'ma Subscription Information

Please enter my subscription to *Sh'ma: A Journal of Jewish Responsibility*.

SUBSCRIPTION FOR: __ 2 YEARS AT $36 __ 1 YEAR AT $21

Name/Address:_____

_____

_____

Telephone: _____

Email Address: _____

Total enclosed:
$_____

Please mail, with check made payable to *Sh'ma*, to:
P.O. Box 1019 Manchester, NH 03105

Living Words V: The Best High Holiday Sermons of 5763

Sh'ma is planning to publish Living Words each year, recording the issues of the year and the passions of the season. We would love to consider one of your sermons, either a sermon you delivered or a sermon you heard, for inclusion in this collection. Please complete the following form and return it to our office next fall with a "best" sermon of your choice.

Sermon title:

Theme of sermon:

Submitted by:
Name: _____

Address: number & street _____

City _____State _____ Zip Code_____

Email: _____

Telephone Number: _____

I would also like to advance-order a copy of *Living Words/Sermons of 5763* at the reduced cost of $18.00 (including shipping and handling).
Enclosed is $_____ for _____copies

Please send to:
Name _____
Address _____
Email _____

Return with check, made payable to *Sh'ma*, to
POB 9129, Newton Upper Falls, MA 02464

Jewish Family & Life!, the publisher of *Sh'ma*, also produces these projects, including web magazines, distance learning, and a new print magazine for middle school students:

JewishFamily.com, the online magazine for Jewish families, provides an inclusive Jewish lens on parenting, food, health, culture, holidays and life-cycle celebrations. The site helps parents integrate Judaism into their daily lives.

MyJewishLearning.com, in partnership with Hebrew College, will provide transdenominational Jewish education and information for users of all educational and ideological backgrounds. The site will offer guided and self-guided learning, an Ask the Experts feature, and discussions.

SocialAction.com is dedicated to Jewish approaches to social justice. With weekly articles and features, learning opportunities, and discussions, this popular 'zine is THE online resource for Jewish activists, volunteers, and organizers.

GenerationJ.com is a hip online magazine for 20- and 30-somethings who have an interest in Judaism but are mostly unaffiliated in a traditional sense. Sections include: lifestyles, relationships, politics, culture, social action, and fiction.

JVibe.com is the premier Jewish teen website, featuring celebrity interviews, music, sexuality, social action, and Jewish culture. JVibe is an accepting community of teens devoted to pluralism, tikkun olam, and everything cool. Sister site Mz.Vibe.com is the online home for Jewish feminist teens.

BabagaNewz is a joint venture with the AVI CHAI Foundation, targeted to middle school students in Jewish day and supplementary schools. The centerpiece is a monthly, print magazine developed around Jewish values. Also included are a book club, web site, and teacher's guide.

JSkyway.com, a partnership with JESNA, provides professional development programming to middle school teachers in Jewish day schools using a combination of scheduled asynchronous distance learning and high-quality, web-based, synchronous videoconferencing.

JBooks.com is dedicated to the idea that books are enhancing the Jewish spiritual renaissance. JBooks.com enriches books coverage by publishing reviews addressing the interests of a diverse Jewish community.

JewZ.com: Jewish Family & Life! and the Jewish Television Network have teamed up to create this dynamic new portal for Jewish information, currently reaching over a million households every week, and have 3 television shows on PBS in 70 major communities.

InterfaithFamily.com, produced by JFL's independent affiliate InterfaithFamily.com, Inc., is the online resource and community where interfaith families exploring Jewish life find the helpful, welcoming information they want and need.

CHECK OUT OTHER GREAT JFL BOOKS!

*my*Jewish Learning.com

The Personal Gateway to Jewish Exploration

MyJewishLearning.com will be a comprehensive trans-denominational adult Jewish learning Website created for people with varying levels of Jewish knowledge, from rudimentary to advanced, covering Jewish holidays, rituals, lifecycle events, texts, history, culture, and ideas and beliefs.

An exciting new joint initiative between

HEBREW COLLEGE

www.JFLMedia.com